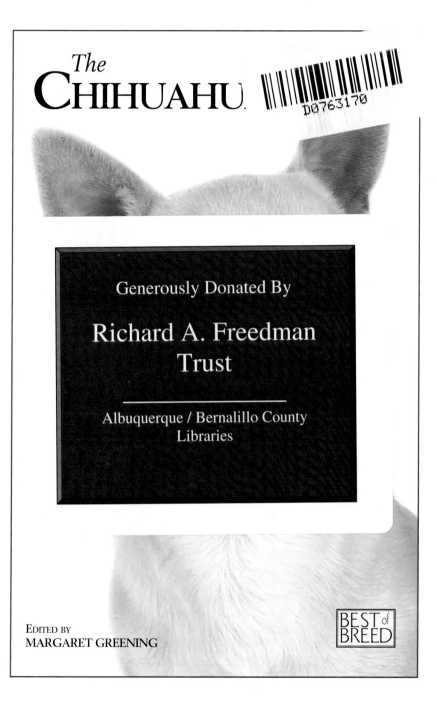

The CHIHUAHU.

EDITED BY
MARGARET GREENING

BEST of BREED

ACKNOWLEDGEMENTS

The publishers would like to thank the following for help with photography: Margaret Greening (Hamaja); Shirley Orme (Ormslet); Pat Milton (Cleopy); Pat Cullen (Culcia); David Milton (Gestavo); Graham Foote (Ballybroke); Shelda Hornby (Bramerita); Linda George (Ouachitah); Hearing Dogs for Deaf People; Pets As Therapy.

Cover photo: © Tracy Morgan Animal Photography (www.animalphotographer.co.uk)
Dog featured is Stepheter Willy Nilly of Hamaja ShCM, owned by Margaret Greening.

Page 16 © istockphoto.com/Anna Utekhina; Pages 42 and 43 © istockphoto.com/Eric Isselée

The British Breed Standard reproduced in Chapter 7 is the copyright of the Kennel Club and published with the club's kind permission. Extracts from the American Breed Standard are reproduced by kind permission of the American Kennel Club.

THE QUESTION OF GENDER
The 'he' pronoun is used throughout this book instead of the rather impersonal 'it',
but no gender bias is intended.

First published in 2011 by The Pet Book Publishing Company Limited
The Old Hen House, St Martin's Farm, Zeals, Warminster, BA12 6NZ, UK
Reprinted in 2014

ISBN
978-1-910488-15-7
1-910488-15-1

Printed by Printworks Global Ltd. London & Hong Kong

CONTENTS

GETTING TO KNOW CHIHUAHUAS

Chapter 1

This tiny breed – the smallest of all dogs – is bright, alert, inquisitive, loyal and affectionate. This is a breed that is big on personality and refuses to accept that it is a tiny dog. It is ready to take on the world. Like most of the Toy breeds, the Chihuahua is considered to be a companion dog and comes under the umbrella title of being a lap dog. However, most Chihuahuas are extremely sporty and some of them don't terribly like being lap dogs; they are full of life, full of energy and they really do enjoy rushing about and playing as well as appreciating a cuddle on your lap.

PHYSICAL CHARACTERISTICS

Small is beautiful – and in the dog world the Chihuahua is the true miniature. This tiny Toy dog weighs no more than 6 lbs (2.7 kgs), but you would be wrong in thinking that he is slight in build. The Chihuahua is described as "dainty", but this goes with a compact body that is perfectly in proportion. In the Breed Standard, which is a blueprint for

The hallmark of the breed is the head with its well-rounded skull and large, flaring ears.

7

The smoothcoat, generally thought of as the 'original' Chihuahua.

The longcoat has feathering, but it should not be too profuse.

the breed, describing exactly what the Chihuahua should look like, there is no stipulation for height. However, most adult Chihuahuas are around 5 ins (13 cms) tall. The body is slightly longer than the height of the dog, and the hindquarters are surprisingly muscular, which allows the Chihuahua to move briskly and with purpose. When a Chihuahua is on the move, his tail should be carried over the back in the shape of a sickle. The forceful, brisk, jaunty movement is a characteristic of the breed; in showing terms, the Chihuahua should 'own the ring'. A Chi should come in, saying, "I am the best; look at me!"

The hallmark of the breed is the head, which has a well-rounded skull, described as an 'apple' dome'. The Chihuahua is a brachycephalic breed, which is the term used for a short face or short head. Many of the brachycephalic breeds, such as Pugs, Bulldogs, and Shih Tzu, have very 'flattened' faces, with a very short muzzle. This can cause respiratory difficulties, but these are rarely experienced by the Chihuahua, although many have a tendency to snort when they are excited.

The ears are distinctive; they are large and they are held erect when the Chihuahua is alert. When in repose, they flare to the sides at an angle of 45 degrees. The expression is described as "saucy" and this comes from the large, round, dark eyes that are set well apart.

There are two coat types: smoothcoats and longcoats. As far as we know, the original Chihuahua were smoothcoated, and this variety has always has a strong following, particularly in the USA. The longcoated variety was developed later and it also has a devoted following. In the show ring, longcoats and smoothcoats are exhibited in different classes, but apart from the difference in coat, the two types are identical. Many people like longcoats better for pets;

perhaps they are prettier, but the smoothcoated Chihuahua could never be anything but a smoothcoat Chihuahua. Interestingly, the Chihuahua does not have the strong doggy odour that comes from the coat of many dog breeds.

The Chihuahua can be any colour except merle or dappled, but in the UK, creams and fawns are seen most commonly. In the show ring you can win with any colours, though some colours are more favoured than others. Some judges like black and tans – some do not. When a judge is known to favour black and tans, a lot seem to appear in the ring!

In the US, you are more likely to see a range of different colours, which may include cream, fawn, red, chocolate, blue and black.

Patterns and markings seen in American dogs, with or without white markings, include: sable, Irish spotting, piebald, brindle, merle and tan points. In the UK, Canada and Australia merle colouring is no longer allowed, as it is associated with specific health issues, such as blindness and deafness; a similar change is pending in the USA.

SIZE MATTERS

The health of a breed is of paramount importance, and there should be no physical characteristic that becomes so exaggerated that is harmful to a dog's wellbeing. In the UK, the Kennel Club has revised many of its Breed Standards to promote 'fitness for function', which means that a dog should still be

capable of doing the job it was originally bred for.

The Chihuahua was bred to be a companion, so, in one sense, this does not apply. But over the years, there was a tendency for Chihuahuas to become smaller and smaller, and, in fact, the more petite the dog, the more it was prized. However, there are health issues associated with breeding tiny dogs, not the least of which is whelping. If a female is very small, she will struggle to deliver her puppies naturally. The Breed Standard has now been revised and this is gradually being reflected in the size of dogs seen in the show ring.

The Americans have always stipulated a weight not exceeding 6 lbs (2.7 kgs), and now British breeders are encouraged to

THE MOLERA

The Chihuahua has a molera or open fontanelle, which is a unique breed characteristic. It can be felt as a soft spot on the top of the dog's head. In other breeds, and in human babies, the frontal and parietal bones of the cranium fuse soon after birth. But this process may take longer with some Chihuahuas, and in others the bones may never fuse completely, leaving an open fontanelle. Research suggests that the bones will fuse in 50 per cent of Chihuahuas by the age of three.

An open fontanelle is not considered a defect, although it should be fairly small. Chihuahuas with this trait are perfectly healthy, although they should be treated with a little more care, as the head is more vulnerable.

The diminutive size is a hallmark of the breed, but health considerations must always be of paramount importance.

produce dogs up to 6 lbs (2.7 kgs), with a weight of 1.8-2.7 kgs (4-6 lbs) being preferred.

TEMPERAMENT

You may be attracted by the Chihuahua's diminutive size – but watch out for his huge personality! This breed is described as a lap dog, and although he can be very affectionate, he is no pushover. The Chihuahua is alert to everything that is going on, and is always inquisitive. He thrives on having new places to explore, and he always wants to know what is happening on the other side of the fence, or even the other side of the road. For this reason, you need to be vigilant, as the Chihuahua is a great escapologist, and will jump over surprisingly high fences and squeeze through the smallest of gaps if he hears something that might be worth investigating.

This is a breed that thrives on mental stimulation – and it is vital that owners take this on board. A Chihuahua may be small enough to carry around in a bag – but where is the fun for him? The Chihuahua has the confidence to stand on his own four feet, and is more than ready to take on the world. In the American Breed Standard, he is described as "terrier-like" and this refers to his bold and fearless nature.

There is no doubt that the Chihuahua also has a soft side. He is sweet and loving with his family, and will bond very closely with them. He is not a one-person dog; he will share his love among all members of his human family. Visitors to the house will be treated with initial wariness – you will certainly get plenty of vocal warning when strangers are approaching. Despite his size, the Chihuahua sees himself as a formidable watchdog, seemingly unaware that he cannot back up his threats. However, when the noise dies down, the Chihuahua

is open and friendly, and, given the chance, he will enjoy showing off a special party trick, which will bring him lots of attention.

Bred to be a companion, the Chihuahua will be miserable if he cannot spend the majority of time with his beloved family. He likes to be part of everything that is going on; he will use his keen intelligence to try to work out what you are doing, and he will be alert and watchful for any changes in routine. However, when it is time to relax, he will be more than happy to curl up in your lap.

You may sometimes see your Chihuahua quivering; this is rarely a sign that he is cold or frightened; it is breed characteristic signifying that a dog is keen and alert.

As a breeder, I value good temperament above all. It is a fact that most of what we breed goes to pet homes and so a sound temperament must be a top priority. My dogs are happy, friendly and good-natured; they enjoy the company of people and get on well with most dogs. Occasionally at a show, a Chi may feel threatened by a bigger breed in close proximity and will feel the need to stand up for himself. However, in the home situation, a Chihuahua will soon become accustomed to dogs of all shapes and sizes and tend to end up as boss dog!

In general, temperament in Chihuahuas has improved over the years, but we should be aware that a spoilt dog of any size can be a nightmare to live with. Misguided people who buy a Chihuahua because he is "cute" and do not attempt to train him or discipline him may find they end up with dog who rules the roost and is not beyond giving a growl or a nip in order to get his own way.

The Chihuahua is the ultimate 'people dog' and wants nothing more than to spend time with his beloved family.

A LIFETIME'S ADDICTION!

I had my first Chihuahua from my cousin, Lady Margaret Dummond-Hay, when I was expecting my daughter. I was attracted to the breed, as I lived in a very small house and wanted a very small dog. She sold me a bitch, Seggiden Sherry, at a reduced price because I was family!

Sherry had several puppies in her lifetime and still features far back in pedigrees. She was not a show bitch, which I was not aware of at the time – but we all have to start somewhere!

As I had shown and won with my Jersey cattle, I knew a bit about showing, but not much about Chihuahuas, despite having been involved with dogs all my life.

However, Sherry was the starting point of my Hamaja kennel, and now, after nearly 50 years in the breed, I have to confess to being a lifelong addict!

TRAINABILITY

I have referred to the Chihuahua's keen intelligence, and most owners will agree that this is not in doubt. However, you may find the Chihuahua has his own ideas about applying his intelligence. If he can work out an escape route from your garden to see what is going on next door, that is a worthwhile endeavour. But he will not put the same effort into repeating monotonous training exercises, which seem pointless to him.

This does not mean that you should not train your Chihuahua; it just means that you need to be more imaginative so that you make it fun for your clever little dog. In the UK, owners can be quite conservative and would rarely think of competing with their Chihuahua in one of the canine disciplines, such as agility or obedience. But in the USA, Chihuahua owners have achieved a fair degree of success in these fields.

Many owners find that house-training is a struggle, and report that their dogs are not 100 per cent reliable with regard to being clean in the house even when they are fully grown. There is no reason for this, except that the Chihuahua hates the wet and the cold, and may be reluctant to relieve himself outside in these conditions. *For information on house-training, see Chapter Four: The New Arrival.*

With regard to showing, I have had many dogs who loved the ring, and some who did not. If a dog or bitch does not like showing, it is a waste of time and money to go against their wishes – no matter how stunning they look when they are at home. I have found that a bitch is more likely to dislike showing, and I have either found good pet homes or used them for breeding.

The two male Chis I have at the moment adore showing, but those that stand out are Ch. Hamaja Mappa Mundi, who loved every minute in the ring and always knew when we had won, and a bitch called Dryhill Blanchiseusse who would get into her travelling box in the hope that we were going to a show. She always seemed rather bored at home, but she came to life in the ring!

LONGEVITY

We are fortunate that the Chihuahua is a long-lived breed, and many survive well into their teens. It is not unusual for a Chihuahua to reach double figures and still show little sign of ageing. I have known a Chihuahua reach the grand old age of 19 and still enjoy a daily stroll in the garden.

SOARING POPULARITY

Toy breeds in the UK have soared in popularity over the past five years and this seems to have coincided with the trend for celebrities being photographed about town and at world premieres with their dogs. The Chihuahua has seen one of the biggest increases, and this may partly be due to their celebrity owners, which include Paris Hilton, Britney Spears, Scarlett Johansson and Cheryl Cole, to name but a few. The Kennel Club saw registrations of the smoothcoated variety of the breed increase by 206 per cent over five years, jumping from 373 registrations to 1,143 while the popularity of the longhaired variety jumped by 100 per cent in the same period.

The Chihuahua has always

Never under-estimate the intelligence of a Chihuahua.

enjoyed enormous popularity in the USA, where, in 1964, it peaked when it was ranked as the third most popular breed. This was not a good thing for the breed, and those wishing to cash in did not pay due attention to the breed's temperament and breed-related health issues. However, these problems have now been addressed and American Chihuahuas are now much healthier, with the typical Chihuahua temperament. They are now ranked in 12th spot in AKC registrations.

A SUITABLE HOME

The Chihuahua is supremely adaptable and will be equally happy in a palace or a tumble-down shack. This little dog does not mind where he lives as long as he is with his family. If you are living in an apartment, the Chihuahua is ideal because he takes up so little room. However, you do need to be aware of his toileting needs and ensure you have access to exercise areas. If you are a city dweller, you also need to socialise your Chihuahua from an early age so he is calm and confident amid crowds and traffic.

A Chihuahua will also enjoy country life, and will have great fun exploring the garden and going for walks. Again, make sure your garden is escape-proof, as accidents can happen in a matter of seconds if you live on a busy street or on a country lane.

You also need to be aware of safety in the home when you are living with a Chihuahua. Your

A Chihuahua will be happy regardless of whether his home is a tiny apartment or a stately home, as long as he has plenty of company.

little Toy dog is light and athletic and has no problem jumping on to high surfaces – the trouble comes when he decides to jump off. I had a Chihuahua who was quite convinced that she could fly. It was not a good idea and sadly she broke a leg. This did not apparently worry her very much once it was set and it was not noticeable – but the outcome could have been much worse, and it taught me to be extra vigilant.

A Chi is often chosen as a pet by older people, as he is light to pick up and does not need a lot of exercise. However, I would be wary of selling a puppy to an older person unless they had owned a Chihuahua previously. Unless you have experience of the breed – its razor-sharp intelligence and its lightning fast movement – you may be taking on more than you can cope with.

BEWARE!

Unfortunately, in this day and age, because Chihuahuas are so popular and expensive, they get stolen. To this end it is essential that your dog has some form of permanent ID, such as a microchip or a tattoo. Do not leave your Chihuahua in the garden unsupervised if there is easy access to a road. Sadly, there have been a number of cases where dogs – and even whole litters of puppies – have been stolen and lost without a trace.

Security is also important outside the home. If you take your dog in the car, never, ever leave him in it while you go and do your shopping, or go to a restaurant, or any other engagement. Cars are quite easy to break into. If it is hot, you obviously would not leave your dog in a car. But it is more likely that the danger is from somebody helping themselves to a Chihuahua from your car, so if you lifestyle calls for taking your Chihuahua with you, then you must be very careful to keep your dog safe and supervised at all times

PRIZE WRECKERS

Another thing that Chihuahuas seem to do – and they don't grow out of – is prize wrecking! They will chew things; they will tear their toys; in fact, they thoroughly enjoy wrecking anything they can get hold of. If you have a prize wrecker, the secret is to only give toys they cannot destroy. Tuggers and small Kongs stuffed with food are your best bet.

CREATURE COMFORTS

The Chihuahua is a dog that really loves his creature comforts, and, in particular, he likes to be warm. On a sunny day, a Chihuahua will find his own special sunspot and bask in the heat. In the house, he will nestle against cushions and tunnel under towels and blankets. If you have several Chihuahuas, they will often snuggle up together, enjoying the warmth from each other's bodies.

FAMILY CIRCLE

The Chihuahua thrives on human company, and it will not take long for a puppy to find his feet in his new human pack and become an integral member of the family. As well as adapting to any type of home, the Chihuahua

The Chi is a sun worshipper and loves to feel the heat on his body.

will suit people of all ages. He is a fun dog for young couples and he is ideal for older people, as he is easy to manage and will enjoy as much exercise as you are able to give him. With older people, there is only one small note of caution. The Chihuahua is tiny and fast moving, so you need to develop an awareness of where he is at any given time.

Temperamentally, there is no reason why a Chi cannot get on with children. In fact, I have direct experience of this, as my children were brought up with Chihuahuas and my grandchildren have been friends with them from an early age. However, as a general rule, I would suggest that a Chihuahua is not best suited to a family that

has young children. This is a tiny dog that even a small child can pick up, so they are a good deal more vulnerable than larger breeds. As children grow older, a Chihuahua can make an excellent companion, as long as a sense of mutual respect is established.

Children must learn the following rules:
• A Chihuahua is not a toy to be pushed, prodded and picked up at will.
• When he is eating or sleeping he should not be disturbed.
• He should never be teased.
• High-pitched yells and screams should be avoided, as both dog and children become over-excited and situations can escalate out of control.
• Boisterous play with a Chihuahua is not permitted.

A Chihuahua must learn that:
• Children have a higher status in the family pack.
• Instructions coming from children must be obeyed.
• Mouthing or play-biting is not acceptable.

If these rules are followed, there is no reason why a Chihuahua will not fit in perfectly in a family with children.

If you start a family, you need to be careful to integrate your Chihuahua right from the start so he does not feel jealous. With sensitive handling, he will earn to adapt, but this will be a big upheaval in his life – as well as in

A Chihuahua of sound temperament will get on with children, as long as a sense of mutual respect has been established.

yours – and you need to handle the situation with care.

LIVING WITH OTHER DOGS

The Chihuahua is a sociable little dog, and will happily share his life with other dogs. As they are so small, many owners opt to keep more than one Chihuahua, and this rarely causes any friction. Breeders often have a large number of dogs, and the Chihuahua has no problem in finding his place in a pack. If there is a minimum of human interference, it does not take dogs long to work out their relationships with each other and to establish a pecking order.

If you keep several Chihuahuas, you need to bear in mind that they will act as a pack.

I have known a pack of Chis hunt and chase rats and rabbits – and even to kill their quarry. If you decide to keep a number of dogs, it is essential that you establish yourself as leader so that each dog will listen to you and will respect you. *See Chapter Six: Training and Socialisation.*

It is perfectly possible to keep a Chihuahua with a larger breed. I know someone who has Bullmastiffs, and their tiny Chihuahua is the boss of them all. The Chihuahua is utterly fearless and sees no reason why he should not be superior to a bigger dog.

However, in order to establish good 'little and large' relations you need to work hard at supervising initial interactions. It

is all too easy for a big dog to get over-exuberant, and, although he is not intending to be threatening, he can appear pretty intimidating to a dog that is a fraction of his size. The Chihuahua seems to have a long memory, and if he experiences a traumatic incident, such as being bowled over by a big dog, it will stay with him and he may be worried and suspicious in all future encounters.

If you are introducing a big dog, it may be a good idea to hold the Chihuahua on your lap to begin with and allow the other dog to approach and sniff. Give lots of praise to them both, and when you feel the time is right, put your Chihuahua on the floor. Do not interfere unless you are seriously concerned; the dogs need to get to know each other and work out their own relationship.

When you need to go out, do not leave the two dogs alone together, unless at least one of them is in a crate. In time, the two dogs will become the best of friends, but give them both plenty of time to form a bond with each other.

CATS AND SMALL ANIMALS

The adaptable Chihuahua will accept the family cat, and may even become good friends with it. Again, the secret is in their first meetings. If you can supervise these, so the cat is not chased, and, more importantly, the cat does not strike out at the Chihuahua, they will learn to co-exist. It is important to bear in

mind that a Chihuahua is very much on a level with a cat, and could easily be scratched if the cat becomes worried or angry. The Chihuahua has large eyes, and these are particularly vulnerable to this sort of injury.

The best plan is to introduce the cat while your Chihuahua is in his crate. The cat can investigate, while avoiding direct contact. The Chihuahua also has a chance to see the cat – which might be the first time he has seen one. Repeat this a few times, and then allow them to meet when your Chihuahua is out of his crate. Call your Chihuahua to you and reward him, so that he does not become too focused on the cat. It is also important to make sure there is a place of escape for the cat, such as a table or a chair. Keep on supervising meetings, rewarding your

Chihuahua for paying attention to you rather than the cat, and the pair will become accustomed to each other and harmony will prevail.

With regard to small animals, such as hamsters, guinea pigs and birds, the golden rule is not to trust your Chihuahua unless the small pet is safely caged. Instinct can take over in a split second – particularly if you have a pack of Chis – and this is not a fair test for any dog.

EXERCISE

The Chihuahua does not need a routine of regular exercise, which is essential for bigger breeds. He will enjoy playing in the garden, and he will also use up a lot of energy rushing around the house, keeping track of everything that is going on. A Chihuahua will therefore thrive on a minimum of

If initial interactions are carefully supervised, a Chi will learn to live in harmony with the family cat.

The Chihuahua's size and temperament make him an ideal therapy dog.

exercise, but he is also prepared to walk as far you want to go.

I know of one Chihuahua who regularly walks with Bulldogs five miles a day and, in my youth, I had a longcoat who would come with us on major expeditions, trekking up the hills in Wales. Despite his tiny legs, he would reach the top of the hill long before us, and would be there to greet us, saying: "Where have you been? I've been waiting for you!"

The Chihuahua does feel the cold, so he will appreciate being dried after a walk in the rain, and his bed should be located in a warm room where there are no draughts.

THERAPY DOGS
The Chihuahua was bred to be a companion dog, and it is in his

nature to be sensitive to the needs of his human family. This can be developed if a Chihuahua takes on the role of therapy dog. It is now well established that people can derive huge benefits from contact with animals – both physical and psychological – and there are organisations that promote this with great success.

Therapy dogs visit hospitals, care homes, and other institutions with their owners and spend time with the patients and residents. The chance to stroke a dog and chat to his owner has major therapeutic value, and those involved in the scheme find it very rewarding. Therapy dogs also visit schools and help children by encouraging them to talk about dog to handle them, and sometimes to overcome their fear of dogs.

The Chihuahua has made his mark in this field, as he seems to have a special ability to tune into people's feelings and emotions. In this situation, his small size is a bonus, as he can be lifted on to a hospital bed or on to someone's lap with the minimum of effort.

SUMMING UP
The Chihuahua is a truly remarkable animal. He is the smallest dog in the world, yet he has the heart of a lion. He is an alert little watchdog, and he loves nothing more than being with his beloved family. As an owner, you have the responsibility of caring for him and giving him the mental stimulation his keen intelligence deserves. Above all, this is a dog that must be treated like a dog.

THE FIRST CHIHUAHUAS

Chapter 2

The origins of the Chihuahua are shrouded in mystery – a tangle of legend, folklore and documentary evidence. It is not even clear which country the breed came from, as there are two schools of thought, both claiming to know the Chihuahua's true birthplace.

MEXICAN ROOTS

There is strong support for the Chihuahua being the one and only breed that is truly indigenous to the American continent. The hairless breeds associated with Central and South America are thought to have originated in other parts of the world, and the Boston Terrier evolved by crossing other breeds.

The Chihuahua gets its name from the northern part of Mexico, bordering on Texas, Arizona and New Mexico, which bears the same name. But archaeological evidence shows that this tiny dog's history may go back as far as the 5th century AD, and may extend beyond the central and southern regions of Mexico to South America. The Mayan Indians made clay sculptures of small dogs, and these bear a very strong resemblance to the Chihuahua.

In AD1100, Central American Indians, known as Toltecs, conquered the southern and central parts of Mexico, and they kept small dogs known as Techichi, which were quite a bit bigger than the Chihuahua we know today. The Techichi is described as being long legged, with a thin body and a humped back. It is also thought the Techichi had a long coat.

Mexican dog 'overfed to be eaten'. A statuette in the Anthropological Museum, Mexico.

These dogs were kept as pets by the Toltecs, who were highly skilled farmers. They were not working dogs, but were highly valued and were also used in religious ceremonies in the home. There is an additional theory, which has some credence, that the Techichi was crossed with dogs that inhabited the mountains of Chihuahua. These were foraging dogs that lived in holes in the ground. They were known as Perro Chihuahenos.

The next important stage in the Chihuahua's history occurred when the Aztecs conquered the Toltecs and settled in Mexico from 1325 and established their own, unique civilisation, which lasted until 1521.

A SPIRIT GUIDE

The Aztecs had their own religious creed, which included a belief in nine lands. They cremated their dead, and at a cremation they would kill a little yellow or red dog to accompany the dead person on his journey to the afterlife. It was thought that the journey lasted for four years. The dog would reach the ninth land first and would wait on the banks of a river for his master to arrive. As soon as the little dog saw his master, he would swim across and guide him through the dangerous currents and carry him safely to everlasting life. It was said that only yellow dogs could perform this role, and the little dogs would vie with each other to be chosen by their master to accompany him to the underworld.

A skeleton of a fully grown Chihuahua, 1910 in the Natural History Museum, Mexico. It measures 7 ins from nose to tail. Note the molera on the top of the skull, and the three extra molera on the side of the skull.

This explains why many graves excavated in Mexico have contained the skeletons of small dogs.

SPANISH CONQUERORS

The Aztecs were conquered by the Spanish in the 16th century, and it is a matter of speculation as to what happened to the small dogs known as Techichi. Some believe they went feral and survived by hunting small rodents. Others believe they were crossed with the black-and-tan-terrier type dogs that the Spanish brought with them, and this resulted in the first Chihuahuas. We have a gap of more than 300 years, shrouded in mystery, before we get concrete evidence of the breed's development.

THE MEDITERRANEAN THEORY

Some scholars believe that the Chihuahua did not originate in Mexico, but instead came from the Mediterranean. Europe was the home of many types of small

lap dogs, and it could be that the ancestors of the Chihuahua were first established on the island of Malta. It is known that dogs with the molera trait, which is a breed characteristic of the Chihuahua, lived on the island. A molera is like an open fontanelle in a human child – a soft spot on the skull, which eventually fuses together. The Chihuahua is the only breed of dog to have a natural molera. Trading ships would visit Malta on a regular basis and some of the island dogs would have been taken to other parts of Europe.

This theory is substantiated by European paintings of the period, which depict little dogs of the Chihuahua type. However, the most convincing proof that is offered for the Mediterranean Chihuahua is found in the Sistine Chapel in Rome. Sandro Botticelli, the great early Renaissance artist, was commissioned to assist in the decoration of the Sistine Chapel, and he chose to paint a series of frescoes, showing the life story of Moses, which he completed in 1482. Featuring in the frescos is a head study of the little smooth-coated pocket dog of Malta. All of the artists of this period related the events of the Bible to the events of their own time and paid tremendous attention to background detail, using homely objects, such as animals, birds and plants, to convey their message. Dogs frequently represented people. Botticelli was always meticulously careful in his choice of analogy and supporting detail, so it was no mere whim that induced him to place this little pocket dog under the arm of one of the small boys included in the group of Israelites led by Moses when fleeing from slavery in Egypt. The dog in the painting has often been identified as a Chihuahua from Mexico, but the explorer Christopher Columbus did not make his first voyage to the New World until 1492.

It is more likely that dogs from the Mediterranean basin went across from the Mediterranean and North Africa to South America. Thor Heyerdahl with *Kontiki* proved that it was possible. If the dogs were held in high regard by their masters, they would almost certainly have accompanied them – being so small, this would not have been difficult.

DISCOVERING THE CHIHUAHUA

We now take a great leap forward to the 1850s when there is documentary evidence of small dogs living in Mexico. There were long, short (smooth), and even hairless coat types – subsequently known as the Mexican Hairless. Small dogs were taken to the United States where originally they were known as Arizona dogs or Texas dogs, probably because this was the border crossing used to bring the dogs from Mexico to the USA. Later the long coat and the smooth coat varieties were rechristened Mexican Chihuahua after the Mexican state where they were discovered. In 1884 the breed made its showing

Madame Adelina Patti and her Chihuahua, pictured in the 1900s.

debut when it was exhibited in the Miscellaneous Class as a Chihuahua Terrier.

James Watson, a well-known American judge and author of *The Dog Book*, refers to the Chihuahua in 1888, describing them as a small, smooth-coated terriers with a molera and a flat tail. In fact, all the early registered Chihuahuas were smooth-coated, and, to this day, they are regarded as the 'original' Chihuahua.

There is a fascinating account of the Chihuahuas discovered in Mexico, given by Rosini Casselli in 1904. Miss Casselli was a glamorous figure of the time, touring music halls with her troupe of performing Chihuahuas in the early 20th century. She writes:

Of all the canine breeds, there is

probably none so little known or understood as the Chihuahua dogs of Mexico, which were in their natural state a distinctly Mexican race of wild dogs, very shy, and for their size, very savage.

They inhabit only a limited section of the mountainous part of Chihuahua, whence these dogs derive their name. It is believed that these wild dogs are now extinct, although they are reported by the natives to have been seen up to about fifteen years ago [1889], and it is largely possible that they might be found in some undisturbed spot.

These dogs were noted, not only for their extreme smallness, but other peculiarities which they possess.

Their legs are very slender, and their toe-nails very long and strong, and very serviceable to them in making their homes as they lived in holes in the ground.

Apart from their size, their most striking feature was their head, which was very round, and from which projected a very short and pointed nose, and large standing ears; there was also a peculiar skull formation, found only in this race. The hair was short, fine and thick and the wild dogs, even when taken young, could not be domesticated, neither could they live any length of time in captivity.

The Indians, however, had a way of taking these dogs and crossing them with the small specimens of Indian dog, and in this way produced a domesticated Chihuahua dog which was kept replenished from the wild stock as much as possible.

It is impossible to test the authenticity of this account, but it certainly adds interest and colour to the Chihuahua's history.

THE FIRST SHOW DOGS

James Watson was among the first enthusiasts to bring Chihuahuas to the USA. He paid $3 for his first bitch, and she was small enough to fit into a pocket. Sadly, she died from pneumonia. In those early days, the little dogs seemed to have problems acclimatising to the cold winters, which they were not used to. Watson also owned a dog called Manzanita, described as "a red terrier with a flesh-coloured nose, a Pug tail, and a thick, soft coat, but not a long coat." It seems that, at this stage, Chihuahuas were different shapes and sizes, and came in a variety of colours, but they had one characteristic in common – they all had a molera. However, there was growing interest in the breed, and they were exhibited in shows across the USA.

The first Chihuahua to be registered by the American Kennel Club (AKC) was Midget, born in 1903 and owned by H. Rayner of El Paso, Texas. The first Champion was a dog named Beppie, born in February 1903 and registered with the AKC two years later. He was owned and shown by Mrs McLean of New Jersey. Dogs were mostly imported from Mexico, and one of the more influential breeders at

Two Mexican Chihuahuas bred by Senora Dolores de Gonzales in Mexico, pictured in 1950.

this time was Senora Dolores de Gonzales of the Altamira kennels, who began breeding Chihuahuas in 1911 and exported many to the USA and to South America.

In those early days, progress was slow, with 50 Chihuahuas being shown at AKC events in 1916. It was with the establishment of the Chihuahua Club of America in 1923, and the adoption of the first Breed Standard, that put the breed on a firm footing. Among the kennels that made an impact on the breed at this time were: La Rex Doll, Rhodes, Peraltos, and in the 1930s the La Oro line, which was owned by Mrs Ana Vinyard.

Few could have predicted the breed's sensational rise in popularity, reaching an all-time high of 37,000 registrations in 1967 when it was ranked the third most popular breed in the USA.

THE GREAT CARANZA

The first well-known sire in the breed was a dog called Caranza. At the beginning of the 20th century, he was bought, along with a number of other Chihuahuas, by Owen Wister and his friend, Charles Stuart, when they were on a trip to Mexico. The dogs were taken to an old house in Philadelphia, which had Dutch ovens built into the walls. Mrs Ida Garret, one of the great pioneers of the breed, reported visiting the house and finding that the ovens were full of Chihuahua mothers and their puppies. The ovens were kept at the correct temperature by a small wood fire, which was lit in the fireplace.

Sadly, Caranza met with an untimely death on the lands surrounding the house. A great storm had swept across Philadelphia and a great oak tree was blown down. Caranza went to investigate, but when he was running along the trunk of the fallen tree, one of the other dogs – an elderly Great Dane with failing eyesight – mistook his little friend for a squirrel and grabbed him by the neck and killed him.

Fortunately, this was not before Caranza had left his mark on the breed as a highly successful sire. Interestingly, there are only two names on his pedigree – Duke and Deano, his sire and dam. Neither of these are Mexican names, which leads to speculation as to whether he was a purebed Mexican dog. He was described as being dark red with ruby eyes, a long coat, a tail like a squirrel, and long ear fringes. He was longer in the body than his height at the withers, and weighed about 3 lbs. The description of his coat is also interesting, as all the dogs coming out of Mexico at this time were smoothcoated. However, there is no doubting the tremendous influence that Caranza had on the breed in the USA. Two great families of American Chihuahua sprang from this little dog – Meron and Perrito.

Mrs Ida Garrett was behind the Meron kennel and she did much to promote the breed. She produced many great Champions: the first was Ch. Little Meron, a fawn, smoothcoated dog with cream shadings.

ARRIVING IN BRITAIN

There are records of Chihuahua being kept as pets in Britain as early as 1850. Hilary Harmar, a world authority on Toy dogs who also bred Chihuahuas, reported that she was presented with two stuffed Chihuahuas at Crufts 1959. She writes:

Hilary Harmar with her Chihuahuas, one of the pioneers of the breed in Britain.

They are typical of Chihuahua of those days (about 1880), and probably weighed about 5 lb. They have very large ears, rather long, pointed muzzles, enormous eyes and very curious long feet with the typical curved nails.

In 1895, the Ladies Kennel Association held the first show organised by ladies, for ladies. It was held at the Ranleigh Gardens and it is recorded that Lady Firbank exhibited a Chihuahua called Theo. But it was not until 1907 that the first Chihuahua

was registered by the Kennel Club. This was a sable, smoothcoated bitch called Topsy. There was a long gap until 1924 when the next Chihuahua, a black-and-tan dog called Sorta Solo, was registered. The development of the breed was slow in those early years, with only 59 Chihuahuas registered between 1907 and 1940.

THE BREED DEVELOPS

The first longcoated Chihuahuas arrived in Britain in the early 1950s; they were Ch. Cholderton Little Scampy of Teeny Wee and Ch. Nellistar Schaefer's Taffy Boy. Until then, it was only smoothcoated Chihuahuas that had been imported.

Mrs Gott was instrumental in developing the breed, with imports from Major Mundey's kennel in Mexico, which included an apricot fawn bitch called Tarahumara, and a male called Tolteca, a white dog with fawn patches, who proved to be a prolific sire.

Mrs Gott also imported a number of dogs from Mrs Stock's Sunstock kennel in California, USA. They included Sunstock Jollo and Sunstock Systy. Later, Mrs Gott established her own

Ch. Cholderton Little Scampy of Teeny Wee: The first longcoated Chihuahua to arrive in the UK.

The first Challenge Certificates awarded to Chihuahua: Left, Ch. Bowerhinton Isabela and right Ch. Rozavel Diaz.

kennel name, Munsun, combining the names of Mundey and Sunstock.

The year 1953 proved to be a landmark when the first Chihuahua Champion was made up in Britain. This was Ch. Rozavel Diaz. He was one of three males born in quarantine to Rozavel La Ora Sena de Ora who had been imported by Mrs Thelma Gray from Mrs Anna Vinyard's La Ora kennel in Cincinnati, Ohio. This bitch was a daughter of the International Ch. La Ora Alino de Tortilla de Ora. This was the first of many Rozavel Chihuahuas to make their mark in the show ring. The first female Champion was Ch. Bowerhinton Isabela.

The other significant British kennels operating at this time were: Palace Court, Brownridge, Hacienda, Kelsboro, Dalhaboch,

Seggiden, Rozavel and Rowley. Many of the Chihuahuas today trace their roots back to these kennels and to the dogs they imported from the USA.

THE TWO VARIETIES

Longcoated and smoothcoated Chihuahuas were shown together in the USA until 1952 when the longcoat was made a separate variety. The first longcoat club was established 50 years after the first Chihuahua registrations in the US. Initially longcoats were allowed to be 2 lbs heavier (0.9 kgs) – up to 8 lbs (3.6 kgs) in weight – but this was later revised.

In the UK, the varieties were not separated until 1965. Some of the longcoats came in from the US and some were developed in the UK. There is no written evidence, but it is strongly

suggested that other Toy dogs, such as Papillons and Pomeranians, were used to establish the coats of the Chihuahuas, and even today you can see signs of this. The interbreeding took place as late as the 1940s.

The smoothcoat remains the more popular of the two varieties, but both varieties have seen some truly outstanding dogs.

INFLUENTIAL CHIHUAHUAS

In the UK there are a number of leading kennels that have produced some outstanding Chihuahuas in both smoothcoated and longcoated varieties. There are a number that deserve special mention:

CH. ROSABEL TARINA SONG

Winner of Reserve Best in Show at Crufts in 1971, she also went on to win Best in Show at Paignton, the Toy Group at the Scottish Kennel Club, and Reserve Best in Show at the Ladies Kennel Association. In her time, she was breed recordholder.

It was this Chihuahua who brought longcoats to the fore and proved they were capable of winning honours at the highest level.

This little sable bitch, bred by Gilbert and Jean Grevett and shown by Thelma Gray, was described by Vera Gillott (Yetagen) as being "beautifully constructed with no exaggerations". Graham Foote (Ballybroke) attributed her big wins to her correct conformation, excellent movement and her "enormous personality".

CH. BELMURIZ BREVIER

Winner of Reserve Best in Show at Crufts in 1979, three Best in Show awards at general Championship shows, and winner of 36 Challenge Certificates. This fawn dog, owned and bred by Carrie Murray, is described by some as being the best smoothcoat of all time, epitomising the Breed Standard.

He was described by Albert Wight (Sharval) as "impish, cocky, brash and filled with such self belief that you could not help smile when you saw him. Fabulous eyes, and correct ears added to his skull shape to give him a head and expression that fanciers strive for. Sturdy in body, stunning in shape and so well-bodied and muscled... truly a

INFLUENTIAL CHIHUAHUAS

Int. Ch Seggieden Jupiter and Int. Ch. Seggieden Tiny Mite.

Ch. Rozavel Tarina Song, owned by Thelma Gray. Winner of Reserve Best in Show, Crufts, 1971.

Ch. Apoco Ballybroke Billy Bunter: A highly influential sire for the breed.

Ch. Ballybroke's Miles Better: A breed record holder with 65 Challenge Certificates.

Ch. Dachida's Master Angel: A prolific winner including four Best of Breed at Crufts.
Photo: Carol Ann Johnson.

Ch. Diella Little Joe: Along with his sister, Ch. Diella Pretty in Pink, this dog was a big winner in the 1990s.

superstar with the style, charisma and magnetism that just made you love him."

CH. APOCO BALLYBROKE BILLY BUNTER

A big winner in the show ring, this sable smoothcoat passed on his winning ways to his progeny with a total of 12 smoothcoat and four longcoat Champions. Most notable were his son, one-time breed recordholder Ch. Apoco Deodar Aristocrat (smoothcoat) and his grandson, Ch. Apoco Deodar Music Man (longcoat).

CH. BALLYBROKE'S MILES BETTER

Breed recordholder with a total of 65 Challenge Certificates and sire of eight Champions. All-round Championship show judge Andrew Brace described this little red dog as "a charismatic showman… his sound, brisk movement always made him an eye-catcher."

CH. TARINA BIANCA

Described as a golden glamour girl with breathtaking beauty, she was one of the top Toy dogs over a two-year period and winner of some 31 Challenge Certificates.

Carol Davies (Dachidas) writes of her: "… a beautiful bitch with classic head and particularly beautiful eyes and expression. Lovely outline, style and conformation, a very classy, sound show girl."

CH. DIELLA PRETTY IN PINK

Alongside her brother, Ch. Diella Little Joe, this bitch dominated the show ring in the 1990s. Winner of 45 Challenge Certificates, she was a top-winning Chihuahua in her time. Graham Foote (Ballybroke) says:

"I find her memorable because of her excellent head qualities, which were not overdone in any way, her lovely profile going around the ring, correct tail carriage and excellent temperament. She always showed off her great qualities to advantage."

Ch. DACHIDA'S MASTER ANGEL

Owned and bred by Carol Davies, who has produced so many good dogs from her top-winning Dachidas kennel, Ch. Dachidas Master Angel has a stunning show record, which includes 52 Challenge Certificates, 13 Groups, three Best in Shows, and three Reserve Best in Shows at all-breed Championship shows. His four Best in Breed wins at Crufts set a new record for the breed.

This blue-fawn smoothcoated

Ch. Bramerita Naughty But Nice: Breed recordholder with an amazing 101 Challenge Certificates.

dog is described by Margaret Greening (Hamaja) as a dog who "excelled in showmanship. With his many Group placings and wins at general Championship shows, he really raised the profile of the breed and made sure it is now taken seriously. He is typey, showy and feisty, and, like most Chihuahua males, afraid of nothing."

CH. BRAMERITA NAUGHTY BUT NICE

This longcoat, bred by Shelda Hornby, has a truly remarkable record, which makes her the top CC-winning Toy Dog and breed recordholder with 92 CCS, 17 times Best in Show at Breed Club/Specialty Shows, and Best of Breed at Crufts in 2002, 2004, 2005 and 2006.

When she won the British Chihuahua Championship Show in 2005, judge Dr Geoffrey Curr wrote of her:

"Distinguishes the great from the merely excellent. Once again, for a magic moment, she filled the ring with a blaze of stardust and we shall have lost something special when it fades."

THE CHIHUAHUA IN THE USA 1950-2000s (Linda George, Ouachitah)

It was the 1950s before a Chihuahua received the top award at an all-breed show, even though the breed had been registered with the American Kennel Club since 1903. In 1951, a smoothcoat bitch, Ch. Attas' Gretchen (breeder/owner Mrs Mike Attas), became the first Chihuahua to win an all-breed Best in Show. She went on to gain two more before being retired. In the mid-50s, the amazing smooth dog, Ch. Tejano Texas Kid (breeder/owner Myrle Roberts), rocked the Chi world by gaining 15 Best In Show awards, a record that stood for 30 years. A total of 10 different Chihuahuas won BIS in the 50s: eight bitches and two dogs, all of them smoothcoats.

LONGCOAT SUCCESS

A longcoat finally triumphed in BIS in the 1970s. The first was the wonderful longcoat bitch, Ch. Snow Bunny d' Casa de Cris (breeder/owner, Martha Hooks). This 2 lb 7 oz fireball captured the heart of seven all-breed BIS judges. She was always breeder/owner handled. This record for a longcoat stood until 1998. The first longcoat dog to be recognised with an all-breed BIS also came in the 1970s with Ch. Flint's Little Lucky Robin getting the nod in 1979.

Am. Ch. Snow Bunny D'Casa De Cris: First longcoat Chihuahua to win a Best in Show.

The 1960s were not so successful for the breed. Only four Chihuahuas won the red, white, and blue BIS rosette at all-breed shows, and then only one each. All of them were smoothcoat bitches. The most notable was probably Ch. Gene's Carla (breeder/owner, Alton Lewis). At the time of her BIS, she had yet to complete her Championship. Such a win "from the classes" is highly unusual in the American dog show world.

In smooths, the decade's most successful dog was Ch. Quantico's Little Crusader (breeder Betty Peterson, owner, breeder and Carol Humphries). Bred in Canada, Crusader won four BIS. Three other smooth dogs and three bitches also achieved BIS awards, one of which was Linda George's first BIS winner, Ch. Quantico's Daisy Mae (breeder Betty Peterson, owner Linda George), also Canadian bred and closely related to Crusader.

THE GOLDEN 80s

The 1980s brought many multiple BIS winners, including the smooth bitches Ch. Call's Delightful Design (five) (breeder/owner Annie Call), and Ch. Jacinta of Evergreen Grove (three) (breeder/owner Liz Johnson). The boys were not to be outdone. Ch. Elh's Mighty Lunar of Dartan (breeders Tanya and Darwin Delaney, owner Sheila Peters) received seven Bests. Ch. Ouachitah For Your Eyes Only (breeder/owner Linda George) won four, Ch. Jo-El's Drummer Boy (breeders/owners Joan and Russ Kruetzman) captured 11, Ch. Holiday Gold Jubilee (breeder Mary Myers, owners Sheila and Mark Weisman) received 16, and Ch. Dartan Strut Your Stuff (breeders Darwin and Tanya Delaney, owners – breeders and Sheila Peters Weisman) took two.

Several of these top-winning dogs were shown over the same time span and competition was intense. On the weekend of

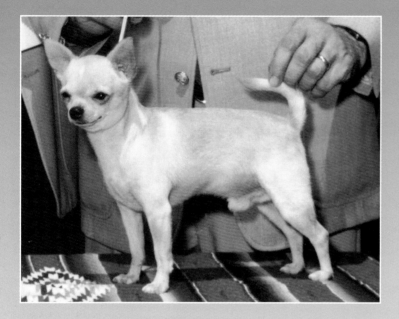

Am. Ch. Jo-El's Drummer Boy: Multiple all-breed BIS winner and four-time winner of the American National Specialty Show.
Photo: Kim Booth Photography.

Am. Ch. Ouachitah Beau Science: Multiple BIS winner and top producing sire in the breed with over 100 Champions.
Photo: Baines Photography.

October 17th, 1986 three different Chihuahuas won BIS. They were; Ch. Jo-El's Drummer Boy, Ch. Holiday Gold Jubilee, and Ch. Jacinta of Evergreen Grove. In the end, Gold Jubilee came out on top for the year, and became the first Chihuahua to be named number one Toy Dog in the country. Of special note, Ch. Ouachitah For Your Eyes Only, aka Snow, (breeder/owner Linda George) became the first and only Chihuahua to ever win the Toy Group at the Westminster Kennel Club show. For many, a Group win at Westminster carries the same prestige as one at Crufts. Unfortunately, Snow was sometimes lukewarm about the show ring, so was shown on a limited basis and retired early.

Longcoats did not fare well through most of the 1980s. It was nine years before another longcoat won BIS. That dog was Ch. Ouachitah Beau Chiene (breeder/owner Linda George), and he achieved two Bests in 1988. Chiene was every breeder's dream dog. Not only did he excel in the show ring, but he became the breed's top producer with over 100 Champions to his

Am. Ch. Bayard Believe It Or Not RJR: Broke a 20-year long BIS record.
Photo: John Ashby Photography.

name, including five that went on to win BIS themselves.

The year 1989 brought the only other longcoat BIS winners of the decade. One was a Chiene son, Ch Bliss Hoosier Boy Named Sue (breeder Elizabeth Bliss, owner Nancy Shapland). The other was a lovely English-bred bitch, Ch. Elandrews Exquisite (breeder Mrs E.S. Gunn, owner Jeffrey Slatkin).

INTO THE 1990s

The most successful smooth during the 1990s was Ch. Ouachitah Rialto (breeder Linda George, owners Dan Greenwald and Bill Andrews), who accumulated 11 red, white, and blue BIS rosettes. One other smoothcoat dog, Ch. Desmond's Ruff N' Tuff E Nuff (breeders Mark and Kathy Lenhart, owner

Mark Lenhart), had two BIS. Two bitches had multiple Bests, Ch. Fresa's Willy Marry Me (five) (breeder/owner Donna Stevens) and Ch. Ouachitah Just One Look gained two (breeder, Mrs Keith Thomas, owners, breeder and Linda George).

In the middle of the decade the amazing longcoat bitch, Ch. Simpatica Celeste (breeder Pat Holzkopf, owners, Mrs Keith Thomas and Linda George), made her appearance. She was a daughter of Beau Chiene, and Linda says she was extremely honoured to have owned and shown her. Linda, and several other longtime and respected breeders, credit Celeste as the finest Chihuahua they have ever seen. She finished her Championship in one weekend with a Group One at six months, five days of age. She won her first BIS before she was seven months old.

Another lovely longcoat, Ch. Bayard Believe It Or Not RJR (breeder Melanie Newell, owners Sam Burke and M.J. Frederickson), debuted at the end of the 1990s and won eight BIS, breaking the record set by Snow Bunny decades earlier. Another longcoat dog had one BIS and two longcoat bitches each had two in the 1990s.

Ch. Nauset I Believe I Can Fly: Top winning Chihuahua in the history of the breed and first long-coated Chihuahua to place in the Group at Westminster.
Photo: Kim Booth Photography.

Am. Ch. Wissfire Chahachi: Multiple BIS winner and Group 3 at Westminster.
Photo: Pat Witter Photography.

THE NEW MILLENNIUM

The 2000s were very good years for Chihuahuas with more records broken. Ch. Nauset I Believe I Can Fly (breeder Mary Jane Frederickson, owners Kathleen Hardison, Erika Lanasa, Ken Saenz, and Mary Jane Frederickson) topped the longcoat record yet again, achieving 25 BIS awards. This beautiful dog also won a Group Three at Westminster, the first time a longcoat was ever seen in the final four Toys at that show. The very next year another longcoat, a bitch this time, Ch. Wissfire Chahachi (breeder Joan Scott, owner Dale Corl), repeated the Group Three win at the same show. Chahachi went on to garner eight BIS awards.

Other multiple BIS winners include Ch. Ouachitah Dangerous Liason (breeder Linda George, owners Dr Ken and Valerie Fox, Wade Davis, and Linda George) with nine, Ch. Emerald Quality Street (breeder Fidelma Dixie, owners Fidelma and George Dixie, Elyse Griffin, and David and Sharon Newcomb with four, Ch. Wil-Cm Paloma Blanca (breeders Curtis Williams, Darlene Wilson and Michael Dunnington, owners Ronald Readmond, Erika Lanasa, and Ken Saenz) with three, Ch. Tradewinds Star Dust (breeder Bert Custodio, owner Ruth Pereira) with four, Ch. Simpatica Mlle Belle Chiene (breeder/

owners Pat and Michael Holzkopf) with two, and Ch. Bell's Hari-Oh of Talisman (breeders Flo Bell, Jill Green, and Alison Gray, owners Flo Bell and Rose Upper) with two. The English-bred dog Ch. Deeruss Flashmoon at Ballybroke (breeder Denise Russell, owner Graham Foote) and five other longcoats each also won a BIS.

In smooths, two bitches and two dogs stood out. The first was Ch. Southfork's Bit-O-Melody (breeder/owner Mary Jane Held) with nine Bests, Ch. Fresa's Willy Marry Me (breeder/owner Donna Stevens) and Ch. Misty Morn Tiramisu (breeder/owner Barbara Solinsky) both with five each, and Ch. South Fork's Banjo Man (breeder/owner Mary Jane Held) with six. Two other dogs had multiple BIS wins: Ch. Bayou's Keeper of the Flame (breeder Carol Pyrkosz, owner Debbie Martin) who earned three, and Ch. Weaver's Defining Moment (breeder Thomas Weaver, owner Megan Boehm) with two. Four smooths each had a single BIS. One of these, Ch. Ouachitah Rio Grande (breeder Linda George, owners Dr. Ken and Valerie Fox and Heidi Spaeth), was the first Chihuahua to have two BIS-winning parents, Ch. Ouachitah Rialto – Ch. Simpatica Celeste.

As we move toward the present, there have been several

Am. Ch. South Fork's Bit-O-Melody: All-time top-winning bitch.
Photo: Kim Booth Photography.

multiple BIS winners in the last couple of years. Some of them are still being campaigned, so in the interest of good sportsmanship they are not included here. The breeders, owners, and handlers of top winning dogs are to be congratulated and thanked. Campaigning a dog to the point where it can win a BIS is time consuming, expensive, and physically demanding for dogs and people alike. It takes tremendous dedication and perseverance to be out there,

driving and showing in all types of conditions, losing as often as winning.

A number of all-breed BIS winners also took the coveted Best of Breed award at the Chihuahua Club of America National Specialty. These include: Ch. Tejano Texas Kid (two), Ch. Jay's Speedy Gonzalles, Ch. Gindon Bo-Jengles of Dartan (breeder Alice Page, owners Darwin Delaney and J.R. Laidley), Ch. Call's Delightful Design, Ch. Holiday's Tijuana La Cune (breeder/owner Mary Meyers), Ch. Ouachitah For Your Eyes Only (three), Ch. Jo-El's Drummer Boy (four), Ch. Bliss Hoosier Boy Named Sue, Ch. Ouachitah Fantasia (breeder Linda George, owner Tom Baldwin), Ch. Simpatica Celeste, Ch. Fresa's Willy Marry Me (four), Ch. Simpatica Mlle Belle Chiene, Ch. Bayard Believe It Or Not RJR, Ch. Nauset I Believe I Can Fly (three), Ch. Weaver's Defining Moment, Ch. Wissfire Chahachi, Ch. Rafina Twist of Fate (breeder Barbara Pendergrass, owners, breeder and Linda George), and Ch. Will-CM Paloma Blanca (two).

We look forward to seeing the future BIS winners and more records being set by top Chihuahuas.

Much of the information included here has come from statistics compiled by the Chihuahua Club of America and published in the CCA Handbooks 1988-2009. Some was taken from Specialty catalogues and some from first-hand experience.

A CHIHUAHUA FOR YOUR LIFESTYLE

Chapter 3

You are making a big commitment when you buy a Chihuahua. This is a dog that thrives on human company, and although your Chihuahua will be quite happy to be left for short periods, you need to work out if you can give him the care and attention he needs.

GIVING TIME

How much time can you give your Chihuahua? Do you work eight hours a day? If you do, you should not be considering any breed, let alone a Chihuahua. In some cases, you may be able to take a well-behaved adult dog to work with you, but if this is not the case, you should wait until your situation changes before taking on a Chihuahua. In most situations, I would suggest that a Chihuahua can be left for two-hour periods – any more than

that and your dog will be miserable. He will put up with times spent apart, but what he wants most is your company.

My experience is that Chihuahuas are really quite nocturnal creatures. They are very happy to sleep in the day and, in the evening, they come to life with a vengeance. My dogs will rush about, play, and jump on to the furniture – so you need to be careful that these sessions do not get out of hand. This is especially important with a puppy who has no sense of danger. You also need to remember that puppies need quiet times when they can rest and grow.

PET SITTING

If you need help looking after your Chihuahua, you could consider the services of a pet-sitter. A dog should never be left on his own for longer than four hours maximum. If you have a

puppy, this is really too long, as you cannot establish a routine of feeding and house-training if your pup is left alone for lengthy periods. You may have a friend or a neighbour nearby who is happy to look after your puppy for an hour or two. There are also professional pet-sitters and dog walkers whom you could employ, as long as you are confident they have experience with Chihuahuas. If you are rehoming an adult, you really do need to be at home most of the time; your dog may well have problems settling into his new home and will need your time and patience.

EXERCISE

As regards exercise, your Chihuahuas will walk as far and as fast as you can – probably further and faster. You have to be careful about free running, as Chihuahuas so not have the best of recalls. Unless you are

A Chihuahua will be miserable if he is left alone for long periods, so bear this in mind before making a commitment.

confident that your Chihuahua will come back, they are better off on the lead. I suggest a daily walk of 20 to 30 minutes, which will keep your dog fit and muscular, as well as giving him mental stimulation. A Chihuahua likes to be treated like a dog – not a child substitute or plaything.

FEEDING

Feeding Chihuahuas is not difficult. I find that mine are prepared to eat pretty well anything – including things you don't really want them to eat. There are plenty of specialist foods for them, so it is not difficult and it is not expensive, but you need to ensure your Chihuahua is getting a well-balanced diet to suit his

individual needs.

For more information, see Chapter Five: The Best of Care.

GROOMING

If you plan to have a smoothcoated Chihuahua, grooming will be minimal. The workload steps up with longcoated dogs, but the basic requirement is to keep the coat free from mats and tangles. In fact, grooming is one of the more pleasurable aspects of owning a Chihuahua, as they love the attention and it helps to build a bond between you and your dog. Brushing is also good for your dog, as it stimulates and massages the skin.

For more information, see Chapter Five: The Best of Care.

SOCIALISATION

When you get your Chihuahua, either puppy or adult, it is very important that you socialise him really well. Get your Chihuahua accustomed to his new home, his family, to noise, to different people, to other dogs, and to different environments. You will never regret spending time on giving your Chihuahua a comprehensive programme of socialisation, as you will be rewarded with a calm, confident dog who is happy to accompany you in all situations. You will also need to allocate some time to training your Chihuahua. You may not have ambitions to produce an obedience Champion, but all dogs – regardless of their size – need a basic education in good manners.

For more information, see Chapter Six: Training and Socialisation.

HOLIDAYS

What about holidays? When you go on holiday, are you prepared to take your dog with you? In the UK, there are places that are quite happy for you to take your dogs as well. A well behaved Chihuahua is nearly always welcome. A lot of these places are self-catering, but you can take dogs to some hotels as well. You may have to pay a slight charge, but not a great deal.

If you plan to holiday abroad, you can take your Chihuahua with you, although it does involve some expense. Your dog will need to be microchipped, vaccinated against rabies, and have a blood test. This will all need to be set up well in advance of your holiday. The best plan is to seek the help of a vet who is familiar with the rules and regulations. On the whole, I would not recommend taking your Chihuhua abroad, particularly if you are only going for a short period of time. There is always a risk that he could pick up a disease or an infection, and I do not believe it is worth the risk.

If you decide to leave your dog at home, you will need to make suitable arrangements. Will a friend be prepared to care for your beloved puppy or adult? This is asking a lot, as Chihuahuas need fairly specialist care. Most Chihuahuas are great escapologists and they do not always come when they are

called. So it is a big responsibility to put on someone else. Boarding kennels are not really suitable for Chihuahuas, as this breed cannot withstand the hurly burly of living alongside lots of bigger dogs. There are people who specialise in looking after Toy breeds in their homes. This is not a cheap option – sometimes I think that boarding the dog is more expensive that the cost of your own holiday – but at least you should be confident that your dog is safe and well looked after.

If you are lucky, your Chihuahua's breeder might be prepared to look after your dog while you go away. I have often looked after dogs I have bred, and they are more than happy to come back to me for a short holiday – they always seem to remember their first home.

FINANCIAL IMPLICATIONS

The initial outlay of buying a Chihuahua is quite substantial, but because of their size, this is not an expensive breed to keep. Obviously, food is a minimal expense, but do not stint on quality – your Chihuahua may be small, but he still needs the essential nutrients provided in a well-balanced diet. If you need to employ someone to help look after your Chihuahua during the working week or when you go on holiday, this needs to be budgeted for. Of course, you hope your Chihuahua will live a long life free from health problems, but you need to be able to pay for medical problems

or emergencies if they arise. You might consider taking out pet insurance to cover these contingencies. You will also need to pay for routine care in terms of vaccinations, worming and flea treatments, which will not be covered by an insurance policy.

The Chihuahua will be delighted to be included in your holiday plans.

You need to decide what you want from your Chi before contacting a breeder.

THE RIGHT CHOICE

What do you want from your Chihuahua? Do you want a companion, or are you hoping to show your dog? Whatever else you plan to do with your Chihuahua, it is important to remember that he will be a pet first and foremost – and we are lucky because we can be sure that the Chihuahua will make a lovely little companion.

If you are buying a Chihuahua solely to be a companion, you do no have to buy from the very top show stock. You want a good-quality, fit, healthy puppy from a reputable breeder. Unfortunately, this may take some finding. The internet has proved to be a growing resource for advertising puppies, but there are a lot of puppies offered for sale that have problems. For example, people are offering crossbreeds when

there is absolutely no need to crossbreed Chihuahuas, or you may find advertisements for 'rare' colours, which are, in fact, incorrect for the breed and not within the stipulations of the Bred Standard. *See Chapter Seven: The Perfect Chihuahua.*

You should also be wary of breeders that offer 'teacup' or 'T-cup' Chihuahuas – there is no such thing! A healthy Chihuahua should weigh 4-6 lbs; an adult dog that weighs less may well have health problems. In fact, puppies that are advertised as T-cup Chihuahuas often grow to full size, or even exceed it.

Sometimes people will sell good-quality puppies, not quite show standard, but happy, healthy pets that are not Kennel Club registered. The puppies are purebred and you will be able to see a full pedigree, but if their

parents are not registered, the puppies cannot be registered. This means you will not be able to show your Chihuahua, and if she is a bitch and you breed from her, you will not be able to register the resulting puppies.

The best plan is to go through your national kennel club where you will get details of breed clubs, and Chihuahua breeders. It is also helpful to go to a dog show where Chihuahua classes are scheduled. This will give you the opportunity to see lots of different Chihuahuas, and you can talk to the exhibitors after they have finished showing. You may find that you have to wait some time before a puppy is available. Reputable breeders often have a waiting list; this may be frustrating if you are eager to bring a Chihuahua into your life, but it is certainly worth waiting if

There is no difference in size between the sexes, so it all comes down to personality.

you know you are going to get a healthy, typical puppy that has been correctly reared.

MALE OR FEMALE?

In larger breeds, the difference in size may be a consideration when you are choosing whether to own a male or a female, but this is not the case with the Chihuahua. However, you will find a difference in temperament, so it will come down to personal preference. Most puppy buyers want a bitch, but, in my experience, males make better pets. They enjoy getting attention, and I have also found that they relate better to women. A female may share these characteristics, but she may be slightly more independent in her outlook. Regardless of your preference, it is important to remember that every Chihuahua

is an individual with its own unique personality.

If you opt for a female, you will have to cope with her seasonal cycle unless you plan to have her neutered. A mature female will come into season every eight to nine months, and during this time you will need to keep her away from males or you will risk an accidental mating.

For information on neutering, see Chapter Five.

LONGCOAT OR SMOOTHCOAT?

Do you want a classic smoothcoated Chihuahua, or do you find the glamorous longcoated variety more appealing? Obviously this comes down to personal preference, and you will find that most owners are passionate about the type they choose. Most breeders will

specialise in one variety, so you will need to bear this in mind when you are tracking down a litter.

The smoothcoat is easy to care for, requiring minimal grooming. The workload steps up with the longcoat, as the feathering will mat and tangle unless it is groomed on a regular basis.

The two varieties have not been interbred for many years, but, very occasionally, a longcoat may appear in a smooth litter, which is the result of a recessive gene. This will be detected by the time the puppies are five weeks old.

WHAT COLOUR?

Chihuahuas come in all colours from white through to black and any variety of any colour. So finding a Chihuahua of the colour that you would like is

The Chi comes in a variety of colours, but you may have a longer wait if you want to choose a more unusual colour.

probably not too difficult. In the show ring, cream, fawn and white tend to be prevalent, although black and tan can be very striking. Colours such as blue do not crop up very often, and may be advertised as 'rare'. However, there are health issues associated with this colour, so it is one to steer clear of. A parti-coloured dog, which has broken patches of colour, is more likely to do well in the American show ring as the Breed Standard allows colours to be "solid, marked or splashed". In the UK, merles are not permitted, and although there is nothing to prohibit parti-colours, they are rarely seen.

MORE THAN ONE?

Chihuahuas are very collectable, and, as they are so small, you may well have the space to keep more than one. However, resist the temptation of buying two pups from the same litter. You are right in thinking that they will enjoy each other's company – but they are more likely to bond with each other than with you. You will need to work very hard, giving each puppy individual time and training, to prevent this happening. If you want to increase your numbers, wait until your first Chihuahua is grown up and mature – at around 18 months – before taking on a new pup.

QUESTIONS TO ASK THE BREEDER

When you have located a breeder who has puppies available, there are a number of questions you should ask before making an appointment to view the litter. These should include the following:

- How many puppies are in the litter?
- What age are they?
- How many males and how many females?
- What colours are there?
- Do you have first choice, or have some of the puppies been chosen already?
- Have the puppies been reared in kennels on in the home?

Resist the temptation of getting two puppies from the same litter.

- When will they be ready to go to their new homes?
- Will the puppies be vaccinated or microchipped before they go to their new homes?
- Will the breeder be available for after-sales advice?

If you want a puppy for showing, you will obviously want to ask many additional questions about the sire and dam's show records and pedigrees.

Do not be put off if you do not get first choice in choosing a puppy. It may well be that the breeder has bred the litter in order to keep a puppy to enhance their own breeding programme, or the owner of the stud dog may get 'pick of the litter' in exchange for the stud fee.

QUESTIONS THE BREEDER WILL ASK YOU

Unfortunately, puppies are sometimes bought by people who do not take into consideration the time and attention that is involved in dog ownership. Sadly, it is the puppy who suffers when he is either abandoned or placed in rescue by a frustrated owner. So all the homework you do in preparation for your pup's arrival will benefit you both.

A caring breeder will ask you many searching questions to ensure you are a suitable owner. These will include the following:

- What is the make-up of your family in terms of those living at home?
- What are your work commitments?
- Do you want to show your Chihuahua or get involved in breeding?
- Do you have other dogs at home?
- Do you have a secure garden?
- Have you owned a Chihuahua previously?

Do not take offence at being asked questions about your

It is important to see the mother with her puppies.

home and lifestyle. The breeder's top priority is to find suitable, lifelong homes for the puppies they have brought into the world. You may find that a breeder is reluctant to sell a puppy to a family that has young children. Chihuahuas get on very well with older children, but an environment with toddlers could prove too hazardous for a tiny dog. Accidents happen all too easily, and a family with small children may do better to opt for a more robust breed.

VIEWING THE LITTER

Ideally, you will be going to see a litter that is reared in the home, as most Chihuahuas are. However, some are kennel reared, and although this is not always a bad thing, you will need to exercise caution. If the litter has had lots of fuss, lots of love and is well socialised in all the different ways – becoming familiar with different noises and meeting lots of people – there is no reason not to go ahead and view the litter. However, if the puppies have missed out on this vital part of their education, you should go elsewhere.

When buying a puppy it is very important to see the mother so you get some idea of how your pup may turn out. You may not be able to see the father, as the breeder will probably have used a stud dog belonging to another breeder who may live at some distance. However, you should be able to see a photograph of him and find out details of his show record. If there are other Chihuahuas related to the litter living with the breeder, ask if you can see them as well. This will add to your knowledge of the type and temperament of dogs that the breeder produces, which will help when you are evaluating the puppies. The Chihuahuas you meet will probably give you quite a vocal greeting, but they should be happy to make friends after a few moments. Beware of

The puppies should be out-going and friendly.

shy or nervous dogs – this temperament is not typical of the Chihuahua.

Regardless of whether the puppies are reared at home or in a kennel, the environment should be clean and smell fresh. The puppies should have a cosy bed, and be provided with a variety of toys. Many breeders use a large playpen to accommodate the puppies during the day, which gives them room to move around freely.

Try to plan your visit to the breeder for a time when the puppies are most likely to be awake and lively – usually before a meal is due.

SIGNS OF GOOD HEALTH

The health of the puppies is of paramount importance, so when you go to visit look for the following signs, which will tell you if they are thriving. The puppies should be:

- Alert and inquisitive.
- Ready to come to you when you approach.
- Well covered but not pot-bellied, which could be an indication of worms.
- Bright-eyed with no sign of discharge.
- Coats should be clean, with no sign of matting, particularly at the rear end, which could indicate diarrhoea.

When you go to see a litter, ask if the parents have had health clearances. Luckily, Chihuahuas are heir to very few ills, but there are some inherited disorders to be aware of. There is a low incidence of heart problems, and occasionally epilepsy seems to occur, but it is in lines that can be identified. Patella luxation, which is a condition where a dog has slipping kneecaps, can be a problem in the breed. *For more information, see Chapter Eight: Happy and Healthy.*

CHOOSING YOUR PUPPY

The breeder may have already booked some puppies when you

Wait until you see a puppy that really appeals to you.

A SHOW PUPPY

If you are hoping to show your Chihuahua, there are many other considerations. You can, of course, show anything – but whether you will win is another matter. Obviously, a top breeder will want to keep the best for himself, so it is not always easy to find a quality puppy with show potential. However, it is important to make your plans known to the breeder, who will help you to assess the puppies. A breeder has a reputation to guard, so it is in his interests to help you select a puppy that has the potential to do well in the ring. When selecting a show puppy, you need to remember that there is no such thing as a certainty, as a puppy can change a great deal as he grows up.

Most breeders will wait until the puppies are eight weeks old before making a full assessment of show potential. The Chihuahua is known as a 'head breed', and therefore this feature is given major consideration. In order to be successful in the show ring, a Chihuahua must have the typical apple-domed head (which will be apparent by the time a puppy is two weeks old), large, lustrous eyes, and large, flaring ears. Ears are the most difficult to assess in a puppy. They are folded at birth, and while they should be erect by eight weeks, they may go through an unsettled stage when the puppy is teething. Despite its size, the body should be strong and sturdy, and, most importantly, it should be in

go to see the litter. If this is the case, do not buy a puppy just for the sake of buying it. Wait until you get the right one, the one you really want. This is vitally important regardless of whether you are buying a puppy with show potential or whether you are choosing a pet. We are fortunate that the Chihuahua is generally a long-lived breed, so you will have a companion for many years. You therefore need to be sure that you choose a dog that will truly suit your lifestyle. Allow the breeder to advise you, particularly if you are choosing a pet. A caring breeder will help to match you with the most suitable puppy, as they will have spent many hours puppy-watching and will know something of the individual temperaments within the litter.

The breeder will help you to assess show potential.

A breeder may be prepared to sell an older dog that is not suitable for the show ring.

proportion. On the move, the puppy should move freely and purposefully – a dog that is put together correctly will move correctly.

If possible, ask a friend who has some knowledge of the breed to accompany you. Two sets of eyes are better than one – and an objective opinion will be of value.

For more information, see Chapter Seven: The Perfect Chihuahua.

AN OLDER DOG

Occasionally, it may be possible to buy a young adult. Maybe the breeder has run it on to show and it is not quite good enough. This may involve a minor fault – for example, a male may not be entire (both testicles descended into the scrotum), or a dog may not have the correct dentition. Or it could be that a dog simply does not like being shown and so will never do well in the ring. Dogs of this type will make

lovely pets and will settle into your home and your lifestyle. In fact, as they are already trained to some extent, it may be a little bit easier for you.

A breeder will sometimes rehome a female after her breeding career is at an end. This is not because the dog is not valued; a breeder will often have a lot of dogs, and believe that a retired Chihuahua will receive more attention in a pet home.

A RESCUED DOG

Taking on a rescued Chi can be a rewarding experience, but it is not always easy. It may be that a Chihuahua needs to be rehomed for perfectly legitimate reasons. It may be due to a marital break-up, a change of job, or it may be because the owner is ill. Because the Chihuahua can be cared for by older people, sadly, the death of an owner can be the reason for rehoming.

On the other side of the coin, there are people who take on a Chihuahua as a fashion whim, or without making a proper commitment, and then give the dog up for rehoming when it becomes too much trouble. A dog in this situation may be neglected; he may not have been looked after properly, and not loved. He may not have been abandoned, but he has not been given the care and attention he deserves.

In most cases, a Chihuahua will adapt well to a new home, given time and patience. However, some dogs may have been badly spoiled by their previous owners and will need retraining before they become a pleasure to live with. You may also get an elderly Chihuahua who has become very set in his ways, and this type of dog needs a lot of love and care to help him to adjust to new owners and a new home.

There are a number of rescue services specifically for Chihuahuas, and, very occasionally, you may find a Chihuahua in an all-breed rescue centre. If you decide to go down this route, the best plan is to contact a rescue organisation and give them your details. When they have a Chihuahua that might suit your situation, you will be contacted. You will be vetted to see if you are suitable to adopt a rescued Chihuahua. In most cases, this will involve a home-check.

Taking on a recued Chihuahua is undoubtedly a big commitment. In fact, it is probably more of a commitment than taking on a puppy. You will have to give your dog more time, more patience and more love, but rescued Chihuahuas do need homes. Your new pet may not look as lovely as a puppy or a young adult, because when we get old we are very often past our best, but don't let this put you off. You can still have a loving, happy pet and can look forward to many years of shared companionship.

With time and paitence you can help a rescued dog to settle in his new home.

SUMMING UP

Once you have bought your Chihuahua home, you are committed to it being part of your lifestyle. You have decided that you want a Chihuahua in your life, so now be prepared for your life to change. You and your Chihuahua will share a unique companionship, and soon it will be second nature to put your dog first. But always remember that even though your Chihuahua is tiny, he is still a dog, so treat him like a dog and you will be rewarded with a friend that is second to none.

Beware! Once a Chihuahua comes into your life, it will never be the same....

THE NEW ARRIVAL

Chapter 4

Before your new Chihuahua's arrival you will need to make advance preparations for his homecoming and ensure that his new surroundings and territory are safe and suitable in all respects.

IN THE HOME

Indoors, it is up to you to decide where you want your Chihuahua to roam but, as a first step, I suggest that you fix a child's gate at the bottom of the stairs to prevent him from going upstairs and then not being able to get down again or, worse still, falling down the stairs. I would also like to issue a particular warning about front doors. Unless you have an absolutely secure front garden, which is rare these days – and garden gates can be left open – the front door must be kept closed at all times. As far as your Chihuahua is concerned, the front door is the road to an exciting new world, full of all sorts of attractions, including cats, passing traffic and the mailman's trousers. I have known too many instances of people's dogs nipping out of the front door and into the road, sometimes with disastrous results. Chihuahuas are not immune to this. On the contrary, despite their size, they are bold, adventurous little creatures and, if it comes to a chase, will usually outrun their owner. If you have a closed porch, the risk is minimised by closing the front porch door before opening the outside door – you just need to get into the habit of doing this.

Homes can be dangerous places. Imagine that you have a crawling baby or a toddler in the house; you would instinctively look around to see what mischief he might get up to and what hidden dangers exist in your everyday surroundings. Chihuahuas, young and old, like the toddler, can be bored, inquisitive, mischievous and greedy, and will tend to sniff, lick and chew anything that intrigues them. Particular likes can be carpet edges, electric cables, house plants (especially if growing in smelly compost), children's toys, paper and cardboard.

In most cases, offenders will cause only minor damage without hurting themselves, but biting through, for example, a TV cable, eating plant fertiliser or polishing off a bar of chocolate could be fatal. Sensible precautions include keeping wires off the floor or covered, choosing your pot plants and fertilisers carefully (see 'In the Garden'), and keeping food and confectionery well out of reach. Remember that Chihuahuas like windowsills and can easily push over a small spindly table. Also be careful about leaving important documents within range – excuses that "the dog ate my homework/licence" are not always untrue!

In assessing the safety of a Chihuahua's surroundings do bear in mind that, small though they are, they can be jumpers and climbers. As a general rule, a Chihuahua can jump to seat height but reaching seat level can be merely a stepping stone to a table top or to the arm of the chair and thence to the windowsill.

Besides minimising the risks of dogs harming themselves because of their innate behavioural traits, the Chihuahua owner must also recognise the dangers of household cleaners commonly used in the home. Did you know that, according to the Environment Protection Agency, 50 per cent of all illness is probably due to indoor pollution caused by the use of cleaning products? You would not let a baby crawl or sleep on a floor recently cleaned with ammonia or bleach-based cleaner, or on a carpet treated with a chemical-based product, nor would you use a room deodoriser or flykiller in his vicinity. Small dogs are equally at risk – in fact, probably more so, bearing in mind that they live their lives closer to the ground than humans and so have closer contact with toxic substances by

Look at your home from a puppy's viewpoint, and try to eliminate potential hazards.

physical contact and inhaling. It is also known that animals have constitutionally more difficulty than humans in eliminating toxins from their systems.

It would therefore seem prudent to improve the atmosphere our Chihuahuas live in by buying cleaners and sprays containing only natural ingredients; these need be no more expensive than chemical-based products.

IN THE GARDEN
You must take great pains to ensure that your garden is

completely escape-proof. Remember that Chihuahuas can squeeze through very small gaps or holes. They are also good at digging. A Chihuahua's motto is: "If I can't go through, I'll go under." So, you will need either to have secure fencing around your whole garden or fence off a secure smaller area within it. All gates opening into areas to which your dog has access – not forgetting any doors or gates at the side of the house connecting the front and rear gardens – should preferably have a spring fastening on them. In addition, they should be securely locked. While a Chihuahua may not be able to open an unlocked gate, a sneaky thief can.

Another good idea is to fix low panels about 12 inches (30.5 cms) high between the gate posts or door sides. These do not need to be particularly strong and can be made from light plywood or rigid plastic. These panels are low enough for you to step over without having to open and close the door on every occasion, while being high enough to stop a Chihuahua jumping over. This is a simple way of controlling his access to forbidden areas and of reducing the risk of accidental escapes.

Garden ponds, fishponds and children's paddling pools are all attractive and pleasurable features to us. To a Chihuahua,

An inquisitive puppy will be on a mission to explore the garden.

Chihuahuas are great escapologists so security must be a top priority.

they are potentially lethal: it can be only a matter of seconds for an inquisitive puppy to fall in and not be able to climb out again. If you have a pond or pool, keep it fenced off or securely netted and always empty paddling pools when not in use.

If household cleaning products can be harmful to Chihuahuas so, to an even greater degree, are the many fertilisers and insecticides commonly used in the garden. Chemical-based products are particularly dangerous; check the warnings on labels and keep your pet away from newly treated areas and plants. While natural soil and plant treatments are generally safer, composts and manure contain hoards of bacteria and

most Chihuahuas are just like most other dogs – they love to gobble up 'muck'. One Chihuahua owner thought she was on to a good thing by using slow-release fertiliser pellets dug into her flower beds, only to discover that her dogs were digging them up and chewing them like Smarties.

Never, of course, use an insect spray while your dog is within range or leave rodent or slug baits where he can reach them. Rodent bait is intended to be attractive to rodents and it is logical to assume that it is therefore attractive to other mammals as well.

Zoologists tell us that animals in the wild learn not to eat plants that are injurious to them, but

domesticated pets have lost some of their natural instincts and may not be able to differentiate between the good and the bad until it is too late. Many plants and shrubs are injurious to dogs; a complete list can be viewed on various websites. There is no need to be ultra-cautious, but if you are buying new plants that you are not certain about, check with the nursery. In general, just keep an eye on your Chihuahua in the garden and if he makes a habit of eating something he should not – get rid of it.

BUYING EQUIPMENT
There are some important purchases you need to make before your Chihuahua arrives in his new home.

SLEEPING QUARTERS

Animals instinctively want their own den; your Chihuahua will be a happier dog if he has a space he can call his own, where he can retreat for a bit of peace and quiet. He will, of course, have his own bed and bedding waiting for him on arrival. The bed can be anything that is suitable for his size, and there are many beds of all shapes, sizes, materials and prices on the market. You cannot ask your pet which he prefers, so you will have to buy whatever pleases you the most. Just remember that your Chihuahua has no aesthetic sense and will be equally happy in an old drawer or cardboard fruit tray (which is easily disposable and replaceable).

All beds need to be cleanable (wood, plastic) or washable.

Foam beds with removable covers are particularly popular with small-pet owners. Whatever you use as a bed, line it with a separate blanket, which can be any sort of material you like, although the fleecy nylon type, which is widely available, is easy to wash and comfortable for your pet.

The advice given earlier about the use of chemical cleaners on floors applies to beds and bedding with even greater force. Your Chihuahua obviously has long periods of intimate body contact with his bedding material and breathes right against it when sleeping. For this reason, it is suggested that you avoid the use of washing detergents and chemical-based cleaning fluids and use only natural products.

The bed should be located in the room where your Chihuahua will spend most of the day and where he will sleep at night. It should be positioned away from draughts; if it is in the kitchen, do not place it next to the cooker, the fridge or any other working appliances. One advantage of Chihuahua owning is that it is easy to carry the bed from room to room if it suits you to do so.

Additionally, it is preferable that your new arrival should have a crate of his own in which you will put his bed. On the one hand, you do not want to imprison him and isolate him from family activity, but a crate does have advantages for both you and your pet. It gives him a refuge to retreat to in order to avoid unwelcome attentions from children or other pets, and he can eat his food in it without

Chihuahuas appreciate their creature comforts; a puppy will need a bed with cosy bedding.

interruptions. From your point of view, you can be confident that your Chihuahua will be safe and not getting up to mischief in your absence. There will also be times when you do not want him running free, such as overnight or when doors are kept open.

The crate should be of open wire mesh so that your dog has full light and visibility, and it should be large enough to allow food and water bowls to be put in it alongside a bed. It need not have a top, provided the sides are high enough to prevent your Chihuahua climbing out. Pet crates can be expensive and you may only want to use one for an initial period until you and your Chihuahua are fully settled into a routine with each other, so, as an alternative, you can fix a single wire panel across a recess or corner.

Newspaper should be put on the floor of the crate. A young puppy will need to relieve himself overnight and if you take on an adult dog, he may not be fully house-trained. Also bear in mind that any animal tends to relieve itself as a way of marking its new territory or because of stress occasioned by his rehoming.

Introduce your new Chihuahua to his crate and bed as soon as you arrive home. Put him in it for short periods and leave the crate door open some of the time. This will encourage him to regard his crate as his personal den and not

A carrier provides a cosy den and is also a safe way to travel.

as a prison. As time goes by and he slides into the household routine, you and he may prefer to leave the crate door open more often, or even permanently. Obviously, the crate can be taken away completely if it no longer serves the purposes for which it was intended.

TRAVELLING BOX/CARRIER
It is worth investing in a carrier, as this is the safest way to transport your Chihuahua. The best type to buy is a manufactured plastic box specifically made for the purpose, which has at least a partial mesh for your dog to look through. This can be secured with seat belts when you are travelling in the car.

FEEDING BOWLS
Fresh water should be freely available at all times. Water and food bowls can be made from virtually anything you like –

pottery, metal, and plastic – the choice is yours. For water, which you will need to change every day, select a bowl that does not tip or slide too easily. Food dishes can be anything from a saucer or some other item out of your kitchen cupboard to an expensive bowl from a pet shop, the only criteria being that your Chihuahua finds it easy to eat out of and does not have to chase it across a slippery floor. It sometimes helps to put a cork or plastic mat under the bowl.

Do not use water containers that are attached to the side of the crate if they have sharp wires. I have known of several serious injuries resulting from the puppy trying to chew the container.

COLLAR AND LEAD
It is essential that the collar you buy is of a size and weight appropriate for the dog. If you are not certain, advice will willingly be given by your breeder, your vet, your local pet shop or by other Chihuahua owners. Some owners who have the larger and heavier types of the breed use a body harness as opposed to a simple collar. At the other extreme a thin halter cord is quite sufficient. If you have bought a puppy, you will, of course, start off with a puppy collar and lead and replace it as he grows bigger.

There is no need for your dog to wear a collar when he is in the house, as it serves no purpose. In fact, most Chihuahuas of my

Unfortunately, Chihuahuas are targeted by dog thieves so you should invest in permanent ID as well as a disc attached to the collar.

acquaintance are always collarless while at home. But there is no reason why your dog should not wear his collar all the time if you prefer this and if he is happy to wear it.

Your Chihuahua will also need a suitable lead; this should be light and slender and can be either a simple cord or a leather strip.

ID

Your Chihuahua must have some form of ID when he goes out in public places. The best plan is to get an identification tag, inscribed with your telephone number and postcode, and attach it to the collar. It is now a legal requirement for your dog to have ID, and these days it really is just not safe to take him out in public without it. He could escape from your arms or out of the car door – and he could fall into the hands of thieves. A name tag will not prevent loss, but it will give you a far greater likelihood of getting your pet back.

I strongly recommend that you have your Chihuahua microchipped as soon as possible, unless the breeder has already done it. Inserting a microchip is a simple procedure carried out by a vet, which consists of injecting a tiny microchip, the size of a grain of rice, into the scruff of the neck. This is perfectly harmless and the dog feels nothing. The identification number is registered by the vet and the chip supplier. Lost dogs can then be scanned by a vet, the police and by dog wardens, and the registered owner can be contacted.

GROOMING EQUIPMENT

The equipment you will need is simple. For smoothcoat Chihuahuas you will need a soft, natural bristle brush; for longcoats you require a hard bristle brush and metal comb. You will also need to buy a toothbrush, toothpaste and nail clippers.

TOYS

There is a wide selection of dog toys you can buy. It may be worth investing in a few in advance, but you may prefer to wait until you have found out what your Chihuahua likes best. Some of my Chihuahuas prefer soft toys, others hard or chewable ones. Put a few in his crate, ready for his arrival, but also keep some outside so that he has something to play with outdoors.

If you give your Chihuahua articles to play with that are not actually manufactured as pet toys (such as old children's toys), you must carefully check them for anything that could be dangerous, particularly glass and plastic eyes, brittle plastic and hidden metal parts. The whole point of toys is to help to prevent boredom, and your Chihuahua will soon let you know what entertains him. So-called 'boredom busters', which contain food substances, are not

Check that toys are 100 per cent safe as a Chihuahua can be surprisingly destructive.

suitable for Chihuahuas, as they can interfere with their digestion.

FINDING A VET

You will need to register your Chihuahua with a vet; you may not need their services immediately, but you never know when your pet may need emergency medical attention and this will be more readily obtained if you have already registered your dog with a veterinary practice.

However, in most cases, you will require veterinary assistance soon after your Chihuahua arrives in his new home. If your puppy has not completed his course of

vaccinations or has not been microchipped, you will need to visit your vet for this purpose. If, on the other hand, you have bought a dog in circumstances in which its origins and history are unknown to you, I would strongly advise that you take him to the vet as soon as possible to have him checked over.

If you have not owned a dog before, you will need to find a vet for the first time. If you want a plumber, your first step is probably to ask friends and contacts for a personal recommendation. So it is with finding a vet; ask around local people who already have a dog and you will not go far wrong. Alternatively, a list of vets in your area can easily be found in local directories or on the internet.

Before engaging a vet, do not be afraid to ask for details of his fees for consultations and for specific treatments, such as neutering and microchipping. Veterinary fees are not regulated and there can be significant differences between one vet's general level of charges and another's.

You may also wish to consider taking out pet insurance at this stage. Your vet, or prospective vet, will be happy to give you details of insurance schemes he recommends or is associated with. Alternatively, you can obtain quotations from a number of insurers online, but in all cases read the small print so that you know exactly what medical conditions and treatments will be covered. Whether or not you take out insurance is, like any health/accident insurance, always a matter of personal choice – and you never know whether you made the right choice until after the event!

At last it is time to collect your puppy.

COLLECTING YOUR PUPPY

When collecting a dog – particularly a puppy – from a breeder, you should be given the following:

- Pedigree registration certificate
- Copy of the pedigree chart
- Diet sheet. This should include a description of the food that the dog is used to, and the times at which he has been fed. A conscientious breeder might also note on the sheet any particular likes or dislikes or eating foibles he may have exhibited
- A small bag of the puppy's usual food, sufficient to last a few days
- Receipt for the money you have paid
- If your Chihuahua has had any vaccinations, you should collect a copy of the vaccination certificate(s), which will bear the name and address of the vet concerned.

If you are buying a puppy from a breeder who is registered with the Kennel Club of England or the equivalent body in the USA, you will also need additional documents to enable you to register your puppy. You will also wish to know whether the dog has been microchipped with a unique identification number: if so, ask for the certificate and transfer form.

THE JOURNEY HOME

The time has now come to take your new Chihuahua home. Use a carrier/travelling box and secure it with your seatbelts. This will ensure your puppy's safety and comfort during the journey. If you do not have a carrier, recruit a helper who can drive or who can hold the puppy on their lap. Remember to provide your passenger with a blanket or towel for obvious reasons!

Remember also that your Chihuahua will have been removed from the environment he has become accustomed to and, in the case of a puppy, from his mother and siblings. Inevitably, he will be stressed; this will be exacerbated by the sounds of the engine, the motion of the car, and other traffic noises. During the journey, your Chihuahua should be confined in the carrier, which should be lined with bedding, or held securely by a passenger, making sure he has a blanket to lie on. This will provide some comfort, as well as soaking up any accidents or car sickness en route. Never allow your Chihuahua to travel without being held or confined. If he is put on a seat, there is a risk that he will either fall off accidentally or, more likely, jump down to find the nearest dark corner.

Under no circumstances should you leave your Chihuahua alone in the car if you need to break your journey. A Chihuahua is an attractive and valuable target and it can take only a few seconds for him to be stolen, even out of a locked car. Carry him with you and, if he not in a box, keep a collar and lead on in case he escapes from your arms or lap.

If the breeder gives you a blanket or toy that your Chihuahua is used to, make sure that he has access to it during the journey. Lastly, but importantly, talk to him: he will be reassured by a comforting voice.

ARRIVING HOME

When you arrive home, give your Chihuahua some breathing space and time to find his feet. Start off by letting him wander in the garden. He will probably need to relieve himself, and, if he does, you can give him lots of praise – making a good start to your house-training.

Next, bring him into the house and let him explore. Resist the temptation of picking him up and carrying him. It is best if he investigates his new surroundings without too much interference.

MEETING THE FAMILY

If you have children, do not let them swamp the new arrival. They will, understandably, be excited and will not realise that loud noises and sudden movements can be frightening to a little creature who is already out of his usual environment. You should explain to young children that their approaches to the new arrival should be slow and gentle: hand movements should be slow and he should be allowed to come to the hand and have a sniff at it in his own time. Children have a natural desire to

pick up a puppy to cuddle him, but they must he urged to restrain themselves until the pup shows he is willing to tolerate such attention. It is not a good start to the relationship if the puppy's first reaction is to snap or growl. Children should be shown the correct way of picking a Chihuahua up, namely with both hands under his ribcage and then with one supporting hand under his bottom – definitely not, as is often seen, with both hands round his tummy, leaving him hanging U-shaped.

If you have obtained an adult by adoption, you may not know your dog's previous experiences and whether any reminders of his past may affect him. For example,

if a dog has been hit, he may dislike his back being touched, or he might cower away from an upraised arm or a broom handle. If he has been shouted at, he may recoil from sudden, loud voices. Other signs may be laying back his ears or showing reluctance to come out of his bed. You will soon learn to recognise any such signs and modify your normal habits until his past recedes from his mind.

A final word, but a very important one, concerning rehomed dogs. They are not instant pets that can be assumed to become the perfect pet on day one. They will normally need a lot of understanding and patience on the new owner's part.

Arriving in a new home is a daunting experience.

An adult dog and a puppy are best left to establish their own relationship without too much outside interference.

MEETING FAMILY PETS

If you already have a dog in the family, keep him away for a short while so the new arrival has the chance to gain a bit of confidence. When the pair meet, you must be on hand to supervise. Remember that although the new arrival may be the apple of your eye, the resident dog may well not share your pleasure – he may even resent the intrusion. Even if they appear to be getting on, you should bear in mind that a boisterous adult can bowl a small puppy over. Also, be careful about showing favouritism: if the new pet gets a welcoming treat, make sure the other dog gets one, too.

THE FIRST MEAL

Your Chihuahua will probably be thirsty when he arrives, so give him his bowl of fresh water immediately. He may also be due a feed, but even if this is not the case, it does no harm to give him a small amount of food to help settle him. There is no cause for concern if he does not eat immediately, but if he still refuses to eat after his scheduled feed time, try to encourage him by offering small morsels by hand.

HOUSE-TRAINING

House-training is a top priority and should start the moment your Chihuahua arrives in his new home. Chihuahuas are no easier or harder to house-train than other breeds, but, given the chance, they will be lazy about it. Some of mine have been happy to perform on the kitchen floor in front of an open back door. One was prone to wee on my husband's shoes (while he was wearing them) and, when admonished, looked up innocently as if to say: "And your problem is…?"

Your dog will usually need to relieve himself at the following times:

- First thing in the morning
- After eating
- After a play session
- After waking up from a nap
- Last thing at night.

In addition, your Chihuahua will need to go out every two hours. If you have a puppy, he should be taken to the garden every hour. Stay with him until he performs and then praise him. Give him encouragement to perform by using a command word or words every time so

Your Chi puppy is bound to miss his littermates for the first few nights.

that he comes to associate the words with the desired action.

WHEN ACCIDENTS HAPPEN
It is inevitable that your new pet will have 'little accidents', although these may sometimes be deliberate to begin with (especially males) as a way of marking their new territory. When these occur, pick up your Chihuahua and put him outside with your usual words of encouragement. A firmly spoken "no" is in order, but you should not scold him in a threatening manner. A Chihuahua that is trained positively is easier to train than a dog that is frightened.

THE FIRST NIGHT
Your new dog may well cry or whine during the first few nights. I leave the radio on during the night for new arrivals and also when the house is empty during the day. I am sure that this provides some company for the puppy and gives him comfort.

I know that many dog owners will not agree with me, but I am not an advocate of dogs sleeping in their owners' bedrooms. If you are of the same mind, start as you mean to go on and do not take your puppy to bed with you "just for the first night or two". Believe me, if you do, you will have him there for the rest of his life. In any event, do not allow a Chihuahua to sleep on the bed. It is not conducive to the wellbeing of such a little dog, who could easily fall off or jump down from bed height.

HANDLING AND GROOMING
You should get your Chihuahua used to being handled as soon as possible by picking him up, stroking and feeling him all over. This will be easy with a puppy, but an older, adopted dog may be slower to accept your attentions and may even initially reject them. Do not worry – with encouragement your dog will come round in time. Here I might mention that it is popularly thought that, because of their size, Chihuahuas are the perfect lap dogs. Sometimes, and to the disappointment of their owners, they do not like lying on laps and prefer to sit and lie beside you rather than on you.

Brush your dog regularly with the correct brush: longcoats

HANDLING

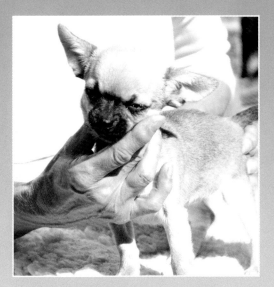

A puppy needs to get used to being handled from an early age.

Check the ears.

Part the lips so you can examine the teeth and gums.

Lift each paw in turn.

If you establish the house rules, your puppy will soon understand what is expected of him.

obviously need more frequent attention than smoothcoats and will also need combing from time to time to remove dead hair from their undercoats.

HOUSE RULES

It is important to decide on house rules and enforce them from day one so that your Chihuahua understands the boundaries as soon as possible. I suggest that your minimum rules should include the following:

- Not demanding to be fed at the table
- No prolonged barking
- Not jumping on the furniture uninvited
- Not jumping up at people. Visitors never like this, even from small Chihuahuas.

Your dog should be trained not to commit these offences with a verbal "no" accompanied by a downwards-facing palm. If your Chihuahua persists then put him in his crate for a short while for some time-out. Above all, be consistent. If you let him get away with bad behaviour on some occasions and not others, it will take all the longer to cure him of his bad habits.

For more information, see Chapter Six: Training and Socialisation.

CAR TRAVEL

A Chihuahua puppy needs a comprehensive programme of socialisation so that he learns to cope with all situations in a calm and confident manner. Early socialisation includes taking your dog in the car, but, unfortunately,

some Chihuahuas seem to suffer from car sickness. If your puppy or adult is experiencing this problem, the best plan is to withhold food before a journey.

If the problem persists, you can try using a DAP (dog appeasing pheromone) spray. You can get bottles of it from the vet and spray it in the car, which will have a calming effect. You can also get medication from the vet, which may help your dog.

SUMMING UP

When a Chihuahua arrives in your home, regardless of whether he is an adult or a puppy, the key message is to start as you mean to go on. If Your Chi understands the house rules, and gets used to your routine, it will not take him long to settle into his new home.

THE BEST OF CARE

Chapter 5

Owning a dog is a commitment that lasts for the duration of the dog's life. You and and your dog have an unspoken pact: he will be your loyal, affectionate friend and companion, and in return you will provide him with love and the best of care for his physical and mental wellbeing. If you do not keep up your side of the bargain, you risk ending up with an unhappy pet with medical and behavioural problems, a result which, apart from being unkind to the animal, defeats your purpose in bringing him into your home in the first place

UNDERSTANDING NUTRITION

As with all mammals, a Chihuahua needs a balanced diet containing the correct proportions of fats, proteins, carbohydrates, vitamins and minerals. The balance of these requirements changes throughout a dog's life. You will start off with puppy diet foods, moving on to foods suitable for adults and veterans – or 'golden oldies' as I call them.

The main elements of good nutrition are:

FATS

These are a primary source of energy for your dog and include essential fatty acids (omega 3 and 6). Fats provide twice as much energy per gram as carbohydrates, and are important for pregnant/lactating bitches and for growing puppies, when an extra source of energy is required. They are also necessary for skin health. Fats come either from animal fats or plant seed oils.

PROTEINS

These are needed for growth, plus tissue maintenance and repair. Proteins are made up of amino acids, some of which cannot be manufactured within the dog's body. Proteins are derived from animals and vegetables, but, for dogs, proteins from animals are more suitable. The best sources of protein are eggs, chicken, lamb and fish.

CARBOHYDRATES

These form the other main source of energy in a dog's diet. There are two types of carbohydrate: simple carbohydrates are found naturally in fruit and vegetables; refined carbohydrates are found in prepared food. Carbohydrates are broken down in the dog's body to form glucose and are transported around the body in the blood. They are found in biscuits, vegetables, rice and pulses.

VITAMINS AND MINERALS

Your Chi's diet must include the range of necessary vitamins, as

A Chihuahua needs a well-balanced diet to suit his age and lifestyle.

the body does not produce them naturally. Each vitamin has a different function and is important for your dog's general health. They are added to complete and tinned foods, and are carefully balanced, as they tend to work in combination with each other. The most important minerals required by dogs are calcium, phosphorous and magnesium.

All these elements need to be provided in the correct quantities and proportions. If you use commercially produced complete foods, you can rely on dietary experts having done the job for you. If you use non-complete foods then you must be sure to provide the right balance of ingredients, particularly when providing vitamins and minerals, as over-supplementation can prove harmful. Dietary advice is available from pet food manufacturers themselves, and, of course, from your vet.

WATER

Fresh drinking water must be available for your Chihuahua at all times. A dog's body is made up of 70 per cent water, and losing just one-tenth of body fluids can be fatal. Water is needed for a number of important functions, which includes: aiding digestion, replacing body fluids that are lost in secretion, and regulating body temperature. If you opt for a complete diet, it is especially important to provide a ready supply of drinking water. Many owners prefer to soak dried food, and this is certainly beneficial for the Chihuahua, who has such a tiny stomach.

CHOOSING A DIET

There is a wide choice of foods available these days, and I suggest that you try a variety of what is available until you find out what your dog likes best and what suits his constitution. For example, you will need to monitor weight, bowel movements and coat condition. Also, but less importantly, you need to choose a diet that is convenient for you and that suits your pocket. I find that Chihuahuas are not much different from children in their likes and dislikes. I know owners whose dogs relish Brand X but spurn Brand Y, while others experience the opposite.

COMPLETE AND NON-COMPLETE

Your main choice will be between a complete and a non-complete food. The former, as its name implies, provides all the essential nutrients your dog needs without adding anything else and is therefore particularly convenient for busy owners. A non-complete food will need supplementing. So, a biscuit meal may need to be mixed with meat; or a canned meat food may need to have meal added to it.

Both complete and non-complete foods may be either dry (in the form of a biscuit type or flake meal) or canned with a high meat content. You must read the labels carefully, and, if in doubt, take advice. Canned foods tend to have a high moisture content, so you need to be sure that your Chihuahua is getting sufficient nourishment if you feed this type of food. Canned foods need to be kept in the fridge once opened.

Dry foods have the advantage of a longer shelf life after being opened and do not need to be kept refrigerated. They are particularly practical for elderly or disabled owners who find opening cans difficult. Some owners feel that dry foods are somewhat boring and lacking in flavour for their pets, but there is no reason why you should not spice them up with a little meat, as long as you do not upset the nutritional balance.

Most complete diet foods have an age-related range, from puppy, through adult and then to older dogs (usually referred to as 'seniors'). Puppies obviously need a high protein content geared to growth whereas, at the other extreme, seniors need only a maintenance food so that they do not put on too much weight. There are also diets provided for pregnant and lactating bitches, and some manufacturers produce prescription diets that may be useful for specific health conditions.

HOMEMADE

You can, of course, give your dog homemade meals and many owners prefer to do so. But bear in mind that there is no point in just filling your dog's stomach. If you lived on nothing but toast, cakes and biscuits, your health would soon suffer, and so would your Chihuahua's. Again, you will have to try out different ingredients and find out what suits him. This is not always as easy as it sounds: some of my Chihuahuas relish and easily digest chicken, while others cannot tolerate it. It is a question of experimenting and making sure that you provide for all your dog's nutritional needs.

FEEDING REGIME

There are basically two methods of feeding your Chihuahua: serving food at set mealtimes, or free feeding, which allows a dog free access to food at all times. Again, the best plan is to find out what suits your Chihuahua. Dogs thrive on routine, so your Chi may well prefer regular mealtimes – this is the regime I use and it has served me well over the years. However, you may find that your dog does not like to eat his food at one 'sitting', and he may do better if he can snack throughout the day. Obviously, free feeding does not work so well if you have a number of dogs, as you cannot monitor how much each dog is getting.

PUPPY FEEDING

Your puppy's breeder should have given you a diet sheet to follow and a small quantity of his usual food to tide him over the first few days. You should also find out how many times a

A complete diet is easy to feed and does not need any supplements.

Canned food is appetising but it generally has a high moisture content.

day he has been fed and at what times of the day. Keep to this feeding regime to begin with. Humans know all about 'holiday tummy' caused by changes of water and food; a Chihuahua's little stomach is even more susceptible to upsets due to sudden diet change. So, if you wish to change your dog's diet or his meal times, do so gradually and be ready to back off for a bit if he shows adverse signs.

ADULT FEEDING

There is no hard-and-fast rule about the number of meals you should give each day. Many Chihuahuas have just one meal a day and this is ample for them; others have two – but more than two is unnecessary. This is really a matter of personal choice for the owner, so long as you do not exceed the recommended daily quantities. If you already have pets then it is obviously more convenient (and less likely to cause friction) if the newcomer fits in with their feeding times.

As regards the daily quantity of food, you should follow the advice in your diet sheet, on food labels and by your vet. In addition, occasional treats during the day are quite in order (see below).

Above all, keep a watch on your Chihuahua's weight: so many canine problems are caused by obesity. You ought to be able to tell by touch and feel if your pet is getting too fat and the remedy is simple and in your own hands.

FOOD TO AVOID

There has been increasing publicity in recent years concerning foods that are harmful, or even poisonous, to dogs, but there is still widespread ignorance about this. So a strong warning – *never* give your dog, or let him have access to, chocolate, apple cores (the pips are poisonous), raisins/sultanas/currants, grapes, mushrooms or onions.

You will need to be particularly on the alert where poisonous foodstuffs may be ingredients in other foods, for example, fruitcake and breakfast cereals. Note also that xylitol (found in sugar-free gums etc.) is also highly toxic to dogs, so check food labelling.

A Chihuahua puppy can only eat small amounts at each mealtime.

HEALTH AND CONDITION

There are two obvious signs to look for if your dog's health and condition is not what it should be: poor coat and obesity.

A dull, greasy or scurfy coat does not necessarily mean that your Chihuahua is on the wrong diet, since there may well be other specific causes. However, it is a warning sign and you should consider his diet and possibly change it to see whether his coat condition improves. If it does not then you will have eliminated one, and probably the main, possible cause so you can move on to a wider diagnosis. If you are concerned about your Chihuahua's condition, seek veterinary advice.

When it comes to evaluating your Chihuahua's weight, think in human terms. A fat, overweight dog is an unhealthy dog. Excess weight puts strains on his legs and organs, leading to problems in later life. Use the bathroom scales to weigh your dog by all means, but a simple pounds weight number will not take you very far. Like humans, Chihuahuas vary considerably in body type: some are small, fine-boned and light, and others are thick-bodied and naturally heavier. Feel your dog's body to see whether there are folds of skin where they ought not to be, such as round the shoulders, and look at his shape to see if he has gained an unduly fat tummy.

Keep a constant check on your Chi's condition to ensure he maintains the correct weight.

TREATING YOUR CHIHUAHUA

Finally, a word or two on the subject of treats. Chihuahuas are particularly appealing little creatures and the temptation to give them frequent tidbits of food is great. "This little bit won't hurt him," is a phrase much-beloved of doting owners, but 'little bits' tend to add up to a significant increase in a dog's total consumption over a period, particularly as tidbits, by their nature, are likely to be heavy on fats, sugar and carbohydrates. You will also find that if treats are offered randomly, at odd times, your Chihuahua will pester you all the time.

Your dog should, of course, have his treats, but make some house rules and stick to them. My dogs have two treats a day, after meals, consisting of a small piece of meat, vegetable or fruit depending on what we are eating. They know what to expect and when, and, consequently, do not ask to be fed at the table or beg for food at other times.

THE SMOOTH COAT

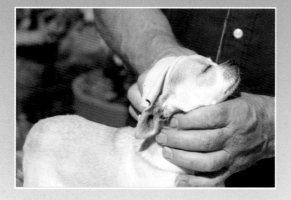

You can bring out the shine in the coat with a chamois leather. This also acts as a massage.

GROOMING

Your Chihuahua will need regular grooming sessions to keep his coat in good order, and also to keep a check on his teeth and nails. It is easier to groom your Chihuahua on a table, both for you and your dog. Bending over a tiny Chihuahua is a back-breaking business, and a Chi is more likely to struggle if he is on the ground. If you are using a table, place a rubber mat or a piece of fleece bedding on the surface so it is not slippery.

COAT CARE

We have a good starting point in that all Chihuahuas love being groomed. If you follow the advice in Chapter Four, you will have accustomed your puppy to being handled from an early age, so he will be calm and relaxed when you need to groom him.

The smoothcoat: This variety is easy to care for, and regular grooming with a soft, bristle brush will keep the coat in good order. The coat should be close-fitting and glossy. The tail – often known as a beaver tail – may have slightly more fur, and there may be a small ruff on the neck. The smoothcoat may or may not have an undercoat. If there is an undercoat, it is woolly in texture. This type tends to shed more than

THE LONG COAT

Use a hard bristle brush and work through the coat layer by layer.

You will then have to comb through the coat.

Pay particular attention to places where the coat is profuse such as on the hindquarters and the feathering on the tail.

those without an undercoat.

Grooming also acts as a massage, helping the circulation, so even if your Chihuahua's coat looks fine, he will still benefit from grooming. Surprisingly, the smoothcoated Chihuahua can shed a lot of hair when he is moulting. This may take place over a period of weeks, or it may happen more quickly. It will help if you use a small pin brush at this stage, which will loosen the dead hair.

The longcoat: This variety will need more frequent grooming to avoid hair tangles. The coat should be soft and it should either lie flat or be slightly wavy. The feathering is on the ears, feet, legs, and on the hindquarters, sometimes referred to as the 'pants'. There should be a large ruff. The tail should be well feathered. An undercoat is desirable, but it should be so dense that it makes the topcoat

fluff out, rather like a Pomeranian.

You will need to use a hard bristle brush and work your way through the coat, paying particular attention to the feathering. You should then go through the coat again, using a metal comb. If the coat is tangled, take time to tease out the knot so that you do not pull the hair, which will hurt your Chihuahua and may cause grooming problems in the future.

BATHING

As a general rule, Chihuahuas do not need to be routinely bathed but you will, of course, have to bath them if they become exceptionally dirty and 'have rolled in something'. If you bath your dog, use a specially formulated dog shampoo, as human shampoos can cause skin problems.

The advantage of the Chihuahua's size is that you can bath him in the sink using a shower appliance. Make sure you use a rubber mat to prevent slipping.

The key to a successful bathtime is to assemble everything you need before you get your dog! You will need the following:
• Dog shampoo
• Conditioner (optional)
• Jug
• Cotton-wool
• Towels

STEP-BY-STEP GUIDE

If you have a longcoated Chihuahua, groom him before bathing him, making sure you comb out any mats or tangles. If you fail to do this, the coat will knot and it will be very difficult to tease out the tangle – and it will be very uncomfortable for your Chihuahua.
• Put cotton-wool in the ears to protect them.
• If you are using conditioner, dilute it in a jug of warm water so you can pour it straight on to the coat. Conditioner is not really necessary for smoothcoats, but if you have a longcoat, it tends to make grooming easier after you have finished bathing.
• Test the water to ensure it is lukewarm and then wet your Chihuahua thoroughly.
• Apply the shampoo, working it into the coat to create a rich lather.
• Rinse thoroughly so there is no trace of shampoo in the coat.
• Apply conditioner, and rinse thoroughly.
• Towel dry your Chihuahua before you get him out of the sink so you absorb most of the moisture. If you have a longcoat, do not rub dry or you will tangle the coat.
• You can allow your Chihuahua to dry naturally, or use a hairdryer (as long as he is used to it), making sure it is on a moderate setting. Brush the coat as you dry it – and, if you have a longcoat, comb through the coat after brushing.

ROUTINE CARE

When you are grooming your Chihuahua, you will also need to carry out some routine care procedure to ensure he is comfortable, clean and healthy.

EYES

The Chihuahua has large eyes, and, because it is a small breed and therefore close to the ground, they can get dust and other debris in them. You will need to keep the eyes clean by wiping away any matter that has accumulated around the lids and corners. Use a separate fresh pad or piece of cotton-wool for each eye and wipe gently from the inside to the outer side.

If the eyes become irritated by dust, they will water, which will inflame the skin under the eye and result in staining. This can be prevented by regular washing, drying underneath the eye and then putting a greasy barrier, such as Vaseline, on the affected area. There is generally no need to use any medicinal eye preparations: if

ROUTINE CARE

The ears should be clean and free from odour.

You may need to trim the hair around the foot on a longcoated Chi.

If you accustom your Chihuahua to having his nails trimmed, he will learn to relax.

anything appears to be wrong, such as frequent eye rubbing, you should consult your vet.

EARS

As a breed, Chihuahuas are not prone to ear problems. Their ears are normally erect, although they may go soft during teething. Inspect your Chihuahua's ears regularly to make sure that they are clean and free from foreign matter. Use a wad of moist cotton-wool or a wipe (there are wipes specially made for dog care) and clean the ear, making sure you do not probe into the ear canal. The inside of the ear should be clean and free from odour. A dog will usually exhibit

signs if there is anything wrong, such as scratching or shaking his head. If you see this, you should consult your vet.

FOOT CARE

Your Chihuahua will need to have his nails trimmed from time to time, but if he runs around regularly on a hard-surfaced yard or path, the nails will tend to wear down naturally. The nail consists of a hard outer cover, which protects the quick (the soft, inner part containing blood vessels and tender nerve endings). If you cut into the quick, it will bleed profusely, which will be painful for your Chihuahua and will probably put

him off subsequent attempts to trim his nails.

If you have no previous experience, you should ask the breeder, your vet, or an experienced friend to show you what to do and what nail length to keep to. You will need to buy nail clippers for dogs; ordinary scissors should never be used. If your Chihuahua has pink nails, the quick is clearly visible, but it cannot be seen on black nails. Therefore, confine trimming to the tip of the nail only.

It is best to accustom your Chihuahua to nail trimming from an early age. Start by lifting up his paws and touching the nails and the pads. Reward him with a

Regular teeth cleaning will prevent decay and keep the gums healthy.

If tartar accumulates on the teeth, you can use a scaler to remove it.

tasty treat when he co-operates. Introduce the nail-clippers and get your dog used to being held steady as you pretend to trim his nails. Reward him handsomely when he is still. If your Chihuahua has accepted these procedures, you can graduate to trimming his nails. To begin with, you will probably find it easier if you enlist the help of an 'assistant', who can hold your Chihuahua.

If you have a longcoated Chihuahua, you will find that long hair grows around the feet, which will become dirty and matted. You will therefore need to trim the hair, following the shape of the foot. Again, do this from an early stage – even if your young Chihuahua has not grown a lot of hair – so that he gets used to it.

TEETH
Regular teeth cleaning is an important part of caring for your Chihuahua. Toy breeds can experience dental problems, so it is especially important to keep a close cheek on your dog's teeth and gums. This is particularly true when your Chihuahua is teething and getting his adult teeth.

It is all too easy for tartar to accumulate in adult dogs, which can lead to gum infections and tooth decay. This is more likely to happen if you feed a 'soft' diet, such as soaked complete food, which will not act as a natural abrasive on the teeth.

If you start early enough, your Chihuahua will accept having his teeth cleaned without undue fuss. The best plan is to accustom your puppy to having his mouth checked. Open his mouth and gently rub your finger on his teeth, so that he learns to accept the intervention without a struggle. You can progress to rubbing some toothpaste on his teeth with your finger. The toothpastes that are formulated for dogs generally have a meaty flavour, so most dogs will be quite happy with this stage of the procedure. Finally, apply some toothpaste on a brush and rub gently. You may find that it is easier to use a finger brush – experiment and see what suits you and your dog. You can also buy dental sticks for your dog to chew, which have the dual purpose of cleaning teeth and providing an occupation.

If you see symptoms such as inflamed gums, mouth odour, loose teeth or bleeding, you should consult your vet.

ANAL GLANDS
Although not strictly grooming, I

will mention here the matter of anal glands. If you see your dog scoot along the floor, this could mean that his anal glands under his tail need emptying of the fluid that accumulates there. This can be a tricky job; some dogs are easier to deal with than others. I recommend that you ask your vet to do it on at least the first occasion. When you have seen what is involved, you can decide whether or not to do it yourself in the future.

THE SHOW DOG

If you are exhibiting a smoothcoated Chihuahua in the show ring, there is little extra you need to do in terms of presentation. A polish with a piece of velvet or a chamois leather will help to bring out the shine in his coat.

In both long coats and smooth coats, a glossy coat is the result of a well-balanced diet and regular grooming, and as long as you have kept up to date with your routine care, your Chihuahua should be in prime condition. There is a little more work involved in showing a longcoated Chihuahua, but this is nothing like the workload involved in exhibiting other longhaired breeds.

The longhaired Chi requires no trimming, beyond tidying up the hair that grows around his feet. The coat must be thoroughly brushed and combed to ensure it is tangle free and looking its best, but in all other respects, the longcoat is easy to prepare for the ring.

NEUTERING

If you have no plans to get involved with breeding, you may want to consider neutering your Chihuahua. This subject is hotly debated, as some owners do not like to interfere with nature. However, there are health benefits that should be considered.

If a male is castrated, he will be less likely to suffer from prostate disorders and the risk of testicular cancer is eliminated. He will also be easier to manage, as he will not be on the look-out for bitches in season. If a female is spayed, she will have a reduced risk of mammary tumours, and the incidence of pyometra (a life-threatening womb infection) is lower. However, this needs to be balanced alongside the risk of putting your Chihuahua under anaesthetic. There is a risk involved in putting any dog under anaesthetic, but the tiny Chihuahua is more vulnerable, and spaying involves more complicated surgery than castration, so a female will need to be under anaesthetic for a longer period.

The best plan is to discuss the pros and cons with your vet and take his advice. In most cases, it is recommended that a male should not be castrated until he is fully mature, at around 18 months. Some vets suggest a female should have her first season before being spayed, but others prefer to do the operation before this time.

A high level of presentation is expected in the show ring.

A Chihuahua will enjoy taking exercise as long as the environment is suitable for him.

EXERCISING YOUR CHIHUAHUA

Most books and articles about dogs rightly stress the need for them to have daily exercise sufficient to keep them fit and healthy, and daily walks are usually recommended. The Chihuahua is a tiny dog and is therefore something of an exception to the rule. Normal activity around the house and garden is sufficient to give your dog all the exercise he needs. This is one of the reasons why they are such suitable pets for the elderly or for people with disabilities, who are less than fully mobile. However, the Chihuahua will also enjoy going for walks, particularly if the terrain is relatively easy for him.

Despite his small size, nothing should deter you from walking your dog if you both enjoy it. Indeed, if you live in an apartment where you have restricted access to an outside area, daily walks might become a necessity.

If you go out walking with your Chihuahua, introduce him to the habit gradually and gently. It is

This is a dog with a lightning fast turn of speed.

probably best to start by carrying him for part of the way until you reach a quiet spot. If he is spooked on his first ventures out with you, by loud traffic noises or unwelcome attention from other dogs, it might be a long job to persuade him to recover from his early, unhappy experiences. On the other hand, when your puppy or adopted adult has become accustomed to the outside world, you may come to realise that the Chihuahua is far from a shrinking violet, and is quite capable of taking on anything several times his size if it has four legs.

CARING FOR THE OLDER DOG

Smaller dog breeds usually live longer than large breeds and Chihuahuas can be expected to have a relatively long life with an extended period of 'old age'. Many articles have been written on the signs and symptoms of canine ageing, but, as with a human relative, you will not have any difficulty in recognising them – it is just a matter of observation and common sense. You will, of course, keep an extra watchful eye on your Chihuahua, but, in general, you should let him live at his own pace. Make sure he gets regular exercise without overdoing it and adjust his food and diet in order to prevent him from becoming too fat. Apart from specific life-threatening ailments, obesity is the condition most likely to shorten his remaining years.

The elderly Chihuahua will enjoy his creature comforts, so make sure your dog has a cosy bed and is never exposed to draughts. This applies to dogs of all ages, but an older dog is more likely to feel the cold. It is also important to dry your dog thoroughly if he gets wet, otherwise he will become chilled, and he may be stiff and uncomfortable when he gets up.

As your dog ages, his eyesight may start to fail. If this happens, make sure you supervise your Chihuahua when he is outside. In the home, try not to move furniture around, so that he does not bump into unexpected obstacles. If your Chihuahua becomes hard of hearing, be patient and considerate with him. You can use hand signals to communicate what you want – you will be surprised at how quickly your Chihuahua learns to respond.

LETTING GO

If you are fortunate (and I use the word deliberately), your Chihuahua will simply pass away one day without any prior noticeable pain or undue discomfort. He has made his own decision that it is time to go, and you have been relieved of the burden of making it for him.

Otherwise, the time will come when you have to decide whether to have your beloved pet put to sleep. A commonly used test for this is to ask: "Has he any quality of life left?" You will probably instinctively know the answer, having observed the telltale signs in your dog, such as ceasing to eat or drink, inability to move, more frequent coughing (if he has a heart problem), and generally looking miserable. You may well wish to consult your vet before deciding, but he can only advise as to your Chihuahua's physical condition, life quality, and probable life expectancy. He cannot and will not make the decision for you – which is yours and yours alone. It is in our nature to want to keep our pets with us as long as possible, but you have to ask yourself whether you want to delay the inevitable

We are fortunate that the Chihuahua is a long-lived breed and many survive well into their teens.

for his sake or for yours.

You will be able to choose whether to have the final act of kindness (which is what it is) carried out in the vet's surgery or at home. Your vet will ask you what your wishes are regarding your pet's body. If you opt for cremation, your vet can arrange this or you can contact a pet crematorium direct. If you prefer burial then you have the choice of doing it in your own garden or arranging, either direct or through your vet, for your Chihuahua to be buried in a pet cemetery.

To begin with, you will miss your Chihuahua terribly, and you will feel that no other dog can fill the gap he has left in your life. It is natural to have a period of grieving. But, in time, you may feel ready to take on another Chihuahua – and in many ways this is the greatest compliment you can pay to your old friend. Remember, every dog is an individual and you will never find a replacement. However, you will take pleasure in the new little character in your life, and also look back on the happy memories of times spent with your first dog. Once you have owned a Chihuahua, you will never want to be without one…

In time you will be able to look back and enjoy the happy memories of love and companionship.

SOCIALISATION & TRAINING

Chapter 6

When you decided to bring a Chihuahua into your life, you probably had dreams of how it was going to be – spending time with an enchanting companion who would give you love, affection and entertainment.

A Chihuahua will do all of this – and more. But a dog, regardless of breed, does not come ready-made, understanding exactly what you want and fitting perfectly into your lifestyle. A Chihuahua has to learn his place in your family and he must discover what is acceptable behaviour.

We have a great starting point in that the Chihuahua has a superb temperament. Bred specifically to be a companion, a Chihuahua asks for nothing more than to be with the people he loves. In return, your duty as an owner is to treat your Chihuahua like a dog. He may be very small – and this is an essential part of his charm – but he is a dog through and through. If you want a fashion accessory to carry in your handbag – buy a soft toy, not a living animal that has his own very special needs.

THE FAMILY PACK

Dogs have been domesticated for some 14,000 years, but luckily for us, they have inherited and retained behaviour from their distant ancestor – the wolf. A Chihuahua has no place in the wild, and we tend to see him exclusively as a Toy dog in a domestic setting. But we need to remember that he has the same genetic inheritance as all breeds of dog, and is born with the mentality of a meat-eating predator who hunts in a pack. A wolf living in a pack owes its existence to mutual co-operation and an acceptance of a hierarchy, as this ensures both food and protection. A domesticated dog living in a family pack has exactly the same outlook. He wants food, companionship and leadership – and it is your job to provide for these needs.

YOUR ROLE

Theories about dog behaviour and methods of training go in and out of fashion, but in reality, nothing has changed from the day when wolves ventured in from the wild to join the family circle. The wolf (and equally the dog) accepts a subservient place in the family pack in return for food and protection. In a dog's eyes, you are his leader and he relies on you to make all the important decisions. This does not mean that you have to act like a dictator or a bully. You are accepted as a leader, without argument, as long as you have

Do you have what it takes to be a firm, fair and consistent leader?

HOW TO BE A GOOD LEADER

When you bring a Chihuahua into your family, the choice of who becomes the leader is up to you to; make sure it is you. Your dog's intuitive quest for dominance, coupled with the fact that it is nearly impossible to look at the palm-size Chihuahua pup and not cave in, gives him an almost unfair advantage in getting the upper hand – don't let him. He will definitely test the waters to see what he can, and cannot, do. Do not give in to those pleading eyes; stand your ground when it comes to discipline. This does not need to be strict or harmful discipline; it is a matter of being firm. It is also important that your Chihuahua is treated in the same way by all members of the family.

There are a number of guidelines to follow to establish yourself in the role of leader in a way that your Chihuahua understands and respects. If you have a puppy, you may think you don't have to take this on board for a few months, but that would be a big mistake. With a Chihuahua it is absolutely essential to start as you mean to go on. The behaviour he learns as a puppy will continue throughout his adult life, which means that undesirable behaviour can be very difficult to rectify.

When your Chihuahua first arrives in his new home, follow these guidelines:
- **Keep it simple:** Decide on the rules you want your

the right credentials.

The first part of the job is easy. You are the provider and you are therefore respected because you supply food. In a Chihuahua's eyes, you must be the ultimate hunter, because a day never goes by when you cannot find food. The second part of the leader's job description is straightforward, but for some reason we find it hard to achieve.

In order for a dog to accept his place in the family pack, he must respect his leader as the decision-maker. A low-ranking pack animal does not question authority; he is perfectly happy to see someone else shoulder the responsibility. Problems will only arise if you cut a poor figure as leader and the dog feels he should mount a challenge for the top-ranking role.

A Chihuahua needs consistent handling from all members of the family.

Chihuahua to obey and always make it 100 per cent clear what is acceptable, and what is unacceptable, behaviour.

- **Be consistent:** If you are not consistent about enforcing rules, how can you expect your Chihuahua to take you seriously? There is nothing worse than allowing your Chihuahua to jump on the sofa one moment and then scolding him the next time he does it because he is muddy. As far as the Chihuahua is concerned, he may as well try it on because he can't predict your reaction. Bear in mind: inconsistency leads to insecurity.

- **Get your timing right:** If you are rewarding your Chihuahua, and equally if you are reprimanding him, you must respond within one to two seconds otherwise the dog will not link his behaviour with your reaction (see page 85).

- **Read your dog's body language:** Find out how to read body language and facial expressions (see page 82) so that you understand your Chihuahua's feelings and intentions.

- **Be aware of your own body language:** You can help your dog to learn by using your body language to communicate with him. For example, if you

want your dog to come to you, open your arms out and look inviting. If you want your dog to stay, use a hand signal (palm flat, facing the dog) so you are effectively 'blocking' his advance.

- **Tone of voice:** Dogs do not speak English; they learn by associating a word with the required action. However, they are very receptive to tone of voice, so you can use your voice to praise him or to correct undesirable behaviour. If you are pleased with your Chihuahua, praise him to the skies in a warm, happy voice. If you want to stop him raiding the bin, use a deep, stern voice

READING BODY LANGUAGE

A confident Chihuahua with bright eyes and erect ears.

This Chi is clearly worried, which he is expressing by turning his head away and pinning back his ears.

The typical tail carriage of an inquisitive Chihuahua who is taking in everthing.

This tail carriage indicates a calm, relaxed Chihuahua.

when you say "No".

- **Give one command only:** If you keep repeating a command, or keeping changing it, your Chihuahua will think you are babbling and will probably ignore you. If your Chihuahua does not respond the first time you ask, make it simple by using a treat to lure him into position and then you can reward him for a correct response.
- **Daily reminders:** A clever Chihuahua is apt to forget his manners from time to time and

an adolescent dog may attempt to push the boundaries (see page 96). Rather than coming down on him like a ton of bricks when he does something wrong, try to prevent bad manners by daily reminders of good manners. For example:

i. Do not let your dog run ahead of you when you are going through a door.
ii. Do not let him leap out of the car the moment you open the door (which could be potentially lethal,

as well as being disrespectful).
iii. Do not let him eat from your hand when you are at the table.
iv. Do not let him run off with a toy at the end of a play session. Your Chihuahua must learn to give up a toy when you ask.

UNDERSTANDING YOUR CHIHUAHUA

Body language is an important means of communication between dogs, which they use to make friends, to assert status and

When two dogs meet they give out clear visual signals to each other.

These two males are showing assertive body language, vying for the position of top dog.

to avoid conflict. It is important to get on your dog's wavelength by understanding his body language and reading his facial expressions. Again, the Chihuahua owner must 'think dog' – even though your dog is tiny, he is still using canine language, which you can read and respond to.

• A positive body posture and a wagging tail indicate a happy, confident dog.
• A crouched body posture with ears back and tail down show that a dog is being submissive.

A dog may do this when he is being told off, or if a more assertive dog approaches him.

• A bold dog will look confident and alert. His ears will be forward and his tail will be held high.
• A dog who raises his hackles (lifting the fur along his topline) is trying to look as scary as possible.
• A playful dog will go down on his front legs while standing on his hind legs in a bow position. This friendly invitation says: "I'm no threat, let's play."

• An assertive, aggressive dog will meet other dogs with a hard stare. If he is challenged, he may bare his teeth and growl and the corners of his mouth will be drawn forward. His ears will be forward and he will appear tense in every muscle.
• A nervous dog will often show aggressive behaviour as a means of self-protection. If threatened, this dog will lower his head and flatten his ears. The corners of his mouth may be drawn back and he may bark or whine.

Most Chihuahuas will view food as a reward that is worth working for.

There are some dogs that prefer a game with a toy.

GIVING REWARDS

Why should your Chihuahua do as you ask? If you follow the guidelines given above, your Chihuahua should respect your authority, but what about the time when he has found a new playmate or discovered a really enticing scent? The answer is that you must always be the most interesting, the most attractive and the most irresistible person in your Chihuahua's eyes. It would be nice to think that you could achieve this by personality alone, but most of us need a little extra help. You need to find out what is the biggest reward for your dog. In most cases, a Chihuahua will be motivated to work for a food reward, but you may find that your dog prefers a game with a toy. If you get into the habit of playing with your Chihuahua from an early age, he will become toy orientated, and will often select a favourite toy. But regardless of whether you are using food or a toy as a reward, make sure it is something that your dog really wants.

When you are teaching a dog a new exercise, you should reward your Chihuahua frequently. When he knows the exercise or command, reward him randomly to keep him on his toes and retain his interest.

If your Chihuahua does something extra special, like responding instantly to a recall, make sure he really knows how pleased you are by giving him a handful of treats or having an extra-long play session. If he gets a bonanza reward, he is more likely to come back on future occasions because you have proved to be even more rewarding than his previous activity.

TOP TREATS

Some trainers grade treats depending on what they are asking the dog to do. A dog may get a low-grade treat (such as a piece of dry food) to reward good behaviour on a random basis, such as sitting when you open a door or allowing you to examine his teeth. High-grade treats (which may be cooked liver, sausage or cheese) may be reserved for training new exercises, or for use in the park when you want a really good recall, for example.

Whatever type of treat you use, you should remember to subtract it from your Chihuahua's daily food ration. It does not take much for a Chihuahua to become overweight, and this will have a detrimental effect on his health and well-being. Fat dogs are lethargic, prone to health problems and will almost certainly have a shorter life expectancy, so reward your Chihuahua, but always keep a check on his figure!

HOW DO DOGS LEARN?

It is not difficult to get inside your Chihuahua's head and understand how he learns, as it is not dissimilar to the way we

When you start training, find an area that is free from distractions so your Chihuahua will focus on you.

learn. Dogs learn by conditioning: they find out that specific behaviours produce specific consequences. This is known as operant conditioning or consequence learning. Consequences have to be immediate or clearly linked to the behaviour, as a dog sees the world in terms of action and result. Dogs will quickly learn if an action has a bad consequence or a good consequence.

Dogs also learn by association. This is known as classical conditioning or association learning. It is the type of learning made famous by Pavlov's experiment with dogs. Pavlov

presented dogs with food and measured their salivary response (how much they drooled). Then he rang a bell just before presenting the food. At first, the dogs did not salivate until the food was presented. But after a while they learnt that the sound of the bell meant that food was coming and so they salivated when they heard the bell. A dog needs to learn the association in order for it to have any meaning. For example, a dog that has never seen a lead before will be completely indifferent to it. A dog that has learnt that a lead means he is going for a walk will get excited the second he sees the lead; he has learnt to associate a lead with a walk.

BE POSITIVE

The most effective method of training dogs is to use their ability to learn by consequence and to teach that the behaviour you want produces a good consequence. For example, if you ask your Chihuahua to "Sit" and reward him with a treat, he will learn that it is worth his while to sit on command because it will lead to a treat. He is far more likely to repeat the behaviour, and the behaviour will become stronger, because it results in a positive outcome. This method of training is known as positive reinforcement and it generally leads to a happy, co-operative dog that is willing to work and a handler who has fun training their dog.

The opposite approach is negative reinforcement. This is far less effective and often results in a poor relationship between dog and owner. In this method of training, you ask your Chihuahua to "Sit" and if he does not respond, you deliver a sharp yank on the training collar or push his rear to the ground. The dog learns that not responding to your command has a bad consequence and he may be less likely to ignore you in the future. However, it may well have a bad consequence for you, too. A dog that is treated in this way may associate harsh handling with the handler and become aggressive or fearful. Instead of establishing a pattern of willing co-operation, you are establishing a relationship built on coercion.

GETTING STARTED

Before you even begin a training programme, you need to be clear about your objectives. It is a common misconception among Toy dog owners that training is not really necessary. If you have a tiny dog, such as a Chihuahua,

THE CLICKER REVOLUTION

Karen Pryor pioneered the technique of clicker training when she was working with dolphins. It is very much a continuation of Pavlov's work and makes full use of association learning. Karen wanted to mark 'correct' behaviour at the precise moment it happened. She found it was impossible to toss a fish to a dolphin when it was in mid-air, when she wanted to reward it. Her aim was to establish a conditioned response so the dolphin knew that it had performed correctly and a reward would follow.

The solution was the clicker: a small matchbox-shaped training aid, with a metal tongue that makes a click when it is pressed. To begin with, the dolphin had to learn that a click meant that food was coming. The dolphin then learnt that it must 'earn' a click in order to get a reward. Clicker training has been used with many different animals, most particularly with dogs, and it has proved hugely successful. It is a great aid for pet owners and is also widely used by professional trainers who are training highly specialised skills.

you are not going to be knocked over if he jumps up, or have your arm pulled out of its socket because he has not learnt to walk on a loose lead. But before you decide you can give training a miss, consider the consequences of having an untrained dog:

- Your Chihuahua will quickly decide he has the upper hand, and will only co-operate when he feels like it.
- He will have no respect for you, and may even try to raise his own status within the family.
- You will miss out on the close bond that comes from spending quality time interacting with your dog.

The Chihuahua is more than capable of mastering the basic training exercises, and if you reward and praise him, he will positively enjoy the experience.

As you train your Chihuahua, you will develop your own techniques as you get to know what motivates him. You may decide to get involved with clicker training or you may prefer to go for a simple command-and-reward formula. It does not matter what form of training you use, as long as it is based on positive methods. Remember to give lots of verbal praise as well

It will not take an intelligent Chi long to learn that a 'click' means a reward will follow.

as rewarding with food.

There are a few important guidelines to bear in mind when you are training your Chihuahua:

- Find a training area that is free from distractions, particularly when you are just starting out.
- Keep training sessions short, especially with young puppies that have a very short attention span.
- Do not train if you are in a bad mood or if you are on a tight schedule – the training session will be doomed to failure.
- If you are using a toy as a reward, make sure it is only available when you are training. In this way it has an added value for your Chihuahua.

- If you are using food treats, make sure they are bite-size and easy to swallow. This is important for all dogs, but most particularly with a tiny Chihuahua. If you have to keep suspending what you are doing every time you give him a treat, it will interrupt the flow of training.
- Do not attempt to train your Chihuahua after he has eaten or soon after returning from exercise. He will either be too full up to care about food treats or too tired to concentrate.
- When you are training, move around your allocated area so that your dog does not think that an exercise can only be performed in one place.
- If your Chihuahua is finding an exercise difficult, try not to get frustrated. Go back a step and praise him for his effort. You will probably find he is more successful when you try again at the next training session.
- If a training session is not going well – either because you are in the wrong frame of mind or the dog is not focusing – ask your Chihuahua to do something you know he can do (such as a trick he enjoys performing) and then you can reward him with a food treat or a play with his favourite toy, ending the session on a happy, positive note.

- Do not train for too long. You need to end a training session on a high, with your Chihuahua wanting more, rather than making him sour by asking too much from him.
- Be patient – the Chihuahua is not going to respond like a work-obsessed Border Collie – but if you make it fun, you will get there!

In the exercises that follow, clicker training is introduced and followed, but all the exercises will work without the use of a clicker.

INTRODUCING A CLICKER

This is easy, and the intelligent Chihuahua will learn about the clicker in record time! It can be combined with attention training, which is a very useful tool and can be used on many different occasions.

- Prepare some treats and go to an area that is free from distractions. Allow your Chihuahua to wander and when he stops to look at you, click and reward by throwing him a treat. This means he will not crowd you, but will go looking for the treat. Repeat a couple of times. If your Chihuahua is very easily distracted, you may need to start this exercise with the dog on a lead.
- After a few clicks, your Chihuahua will understand that if he

hears a click, he will get a treat. He must now learn that he must 'earn' a click. This time, when your Chihuahua looks at you, wait a little longer before clicking and then reward him. If your Chihuahua is on a lead but responding well, try him off the lead.

- When your Chihuahua is working for a click and giving you his attention, you can introduce a cue or command word, such as "Watch". Repeat a few times, using the cue. You now have a Chihuahua that understands the clicker and will give you his attention when you ask him to "Watch".

The Sit can be taught by luring with a treat, and can be reinforced by asking your Chi to "Sit" before he gets his food bowl.

TRAINING EXERCISES

THE SIT

This is the easiest exercise to teach, so it is rewarding for both you and your Chihuahua.

- Choose a tasty treat and hold it just above your puppy's nose. As he looks up at the treat, he will naturally go into the 'Sit'. As soon as he is in position, reward him.
- Repeat the exercise and when your pup understands what you want, introduce the "Sit" command.
- You can practise the Sit exercise at mealtimes by holding out the bowl and waiting for your dog to sit. Most Chihuahuas learn this one very quickly!

THE DOWN

Work hard at this exercise because a reliable 'Down' is useful in many different situations, and an instant 'Down' can be a lifesaver.

- You can start with your dog in a 'Sit', or it is just as effective to teach it when the dog is standing. Hold a treat just below your puppy's nose and slowly lower it towards the ground. The treat acts as a lure and your puppy will follow it, first going down on his forequarters and then bringing his hindquarters down as he tries to get the treat.
- Make sure you close your fist around the treat

An instant response to the "Down" is invaluable.

Make yourself sound exciting so your Chi wants to come to you.

and only reward your puppy with the treat when he is in the correct position. If your puppy is reluctant to go 'Down', you can apply gentle pressure on his shoulders to encourage him to go into the correct position.

- When your puppy is following the treat and going into position, introduce a verbal command.
- Build up this exercise over a period of time, each time waiting a little longer before giving the reward, so the puppy learns to stay in the 'Down' position.

THE RECALL

If you want to exercise your Chihuahua off-lead, you will need to train a reliable recall. The Chihuahua may be small but he is fast moving, and he may find himself in potentially dangerous situations if he does not respond to a recall command. You must teach your Chihuahua that it is fun to come back to you because you are an exciting person and you will reward him with a tasty treat or a game with his favourite toy.

Hopefully, the breeder will have already started recall training by calling the puppies in from outside and rewarding them with some treats scattered on the floor. But even if this has not been the case, you will find that a puppy arriving in his new home is highly responsive. His chief desire is to follow you and be with you. Capitalise on this from day one by getting your pup's attention and calling him to you in a bright, excited tone of voice.

- Practise in the garden. When your puppy is busy exploring, get his attention by calling his name and, as he runs towards you, introduce the verbal

SECRET WEAPON

You can build up a strong recall by using another form of association learning. Buy a whistle and when you are giving your Chihuahua his food, peep on the whistle. You can choose the type of signal you want to give: two short peeps or one long whistle, for example. Within a matter of days, your dog will learn that the sound of the whistle means that food is coming.

Now transfer the lesson outside. Arm yourself with some tasty treats and the whistle. Allow your Chihuahua to run free in the garden and, after a couple of minutes, use the whistle. The dog has already learnt to associate the whistle with food, so he will come towards you.

Immediately reward him with a treat and lots of praise. Repeat the lesson a few times in the garden, so you are confident that your dog is responding before trying it in the park. Make sure you always have some treats in your pocket when you go for a walk and your dog will quickly learn how rewarding it is to come to you.

command "Come". Make sure you sound happy and exciting, so your puppy wants to come to you. When he responds, give him lots of praise.

- If your puppy is slow to respond, try running away a few paces, or jumping up and down. It doesn't matter how silly you look, the key issue is to get your puppy's attention and then make yourself irresistible!
- In a dog's mind, coming when called should be regarded as the best fun because he knows he is always going to be rewarded. Never make the mistake of telling your dog off – no matter how slow he is to respond – as you will undo all

your previous hard work.
- When you call your Chihuahua to you, make sure he comes up close enough to be touched. He must understand that "Come" means that he should come right up to you, otherwise he will think that he can approach and then dart away when it suits him.
- When you are free running your dog, make sure you have his favourite toy or a pocket full of treats so you can reward him at intervals throughout the walk when you call him to you. Do not allow your dog to free run and only call him back at the end of the walk to clip on his lead. An intelligent Chihuahua will soon realise

that the recall means the end of his walk and then end of fun – so who can blame him for not wanting to come back?

TRAINING LINE
This is the equivalent of a very long lead, which you can buy at a pet store, or you can make your own with a length of rope. The training line is attached to your Chihuahua's collar and should be around 15 feet (4.5 metres) in length.

The purpose of the training line is to prevent your Chihuahua from disobeying you so that he never has the chance to get into bad habits. For example, when you call your Chihuahua and he ignores you, you can immediately pick up the end of the training line and call him again. By picking up the line, you will have attracted his attention and if you call in an excited, happy voice, your Chihuahua will come to you. The moment he reaches you, give him a tasty treat so he is instantly rewarded for making the 'right' decision. When you have reinforced the correct behaviour a number of times, your dog will build up a strong recall and you will not need to use a training line.

WALKING ON A LOOSE LEAD

This is a simple exercise, which is neglected by many Chihuahua owners. It is the same old story of thinking that a tiny Toy dog does not need to be trained – and if he is not co-operating, you always have the option of picking him up. But how much better would it be if your little dog walked calmly and confidently on the lead, so you could take him out and about without having to worry about him?

You can use a treat to encourage your Chihuahua to walk with you.

- In the early stages of lead training, allow your puppy to pick his route and follow him. He will get used to the feeling of being 'attached' to you and has no reason to put up any resistance.
- Next, find a toy or a tasty treat and show it to your puppy. Let him follow the treat/toy for a few paces and then reward him.
- Build up the amount of time your pup will walk with you, and, when he is walking nicely by your side, introduce the verbal command "Heel" or "Close". Give lots of praise when your pup is in the correct position.
- When your pup is walking alongside you, keep focusing his attention on you by using his name and then rewarding him when he looks at you. If it is going well, introduce some changes of direction.
- Do not attempt to take your puppy out on the lead until you have mastered the basics at home. You need to be confident that your puppy

accepts the lead and will focus his attention on you, when requested, before you face the challenge of a busy environment.

STAYS

This may not be the most exciting exercise, but it is one of the most useful. There are many occasions when you want your Chihuahua to stay in position, even if it is only for a few seconds. The classic example is when you want your Chihuahua to stay in the back of the car

Build up the Stay exercise in easy stages.

until you have clipped on his lead. Some trainers use the verbal command "Stay" when the dog is to stay in position for an extended period of time and "Wait" if the dog is to stay in position for a few seconds until you give the next command. Other trainers use a universal "Stay" to cover all situations. It all comes down to personal preference, and as long as you are consistent, your dog will understand the command he is given.

• Put your puppy in a 'Sit' or a 'Down' and use a hand signal (flat palm, facing the dog) to show he is to stay in position.

Step a pace away from the dog. Wait a second, step back and reward him. If you have a lively pup, you may find it easier to train this exercise on the lead.

• Repeat the exercise, gradually increasing the distance you can leave your dog. When you return to your dog's side, praise him quietly and release him with a command, such as "OK".

• Remember to keep your body language very still when you are training this exercise and avoid eye contact with your dog. Work on this exercise over a period of time and you will build up a really reliable 'Stay'.

SOCIALISATION

While your Chihuahua is mastering basic obedience exercises, there is other, equally important work to do with him. A Chihuahua is not only becoming a part of your home and family, he is becoming a member of the community. He needs to be able to live in the outside world, coping calmly with every new situation that comes his way. It is your job to introduce him to as many different experiences as possible and to encourage him to behave in an appropriate manner. This is important with all breeds, but it is especially important with a small dog that could easily become worried and nervous when confronted by seemingly daunting situations. A frightened dog is an unhappy dog because he has no sense of security. He may also become anti-social, barking at everything that scares him, as a means of self-protection.

In order to socialise your Chihuahua effectively, it is helpful to understand how his brain is developing and then you will get a perspective on how he sees the world.

CANINE SOCIALISATION
(Birth to 7 weeks)
This is the time when a dog learns how to be a dog. By interacting with his mother and his littermates, a young pup learns about leadership and submission. He learns to read body posture so that he understands the intentions of his mother and his siblings. A puppy that is taken away from his litter too early may always have behavioural problems with other dogs, either being fearful or aggressive.

SOCIALISATION PERIOD
(7 to 12 weeks)
This is the time to get cracking and introduce your Chihuahua puppy to as many different experiences as possible. This includes meeting different people, other dogs and animals, seeing new sights and hearing a range of sounds, from the vacuum cleaner to the roar of traffic. A puppy learns very quickly and what he learns will

stay with him for the rest of his life. This is the best time for a puppy to move to a new home, as he is adaptable and ready to form deep bonds.

FEAR-IMPRINT PERIOD
(8 to 11 weeks)
This occurs during the socialisation period and it can be the cause of problems if it is not handled carefully. If a pup is exposed to a frightening or painful experience, it will lead to lasting impressions. Obviously, you will attempt to avoid

frightening situations, such as your pup being bullied by a bigger dog, or a firework going off, but you cannot always protect your puppy from the unexpected. If your pup has a nasty experience, the best plan is to make light of it and distract him by offering him a treat or a game. The pup will take the lead from you and will be reassured that there is nothing to worry about. If you mollycoddle him and sympathise with him, he is far more likely to retain the memory of his fear.

A puppy learns his first lessons from his mother and his littermates.

SENIORITY PERIOD (12 to 16 weeks)

During this period, your Chihuahua puppy starts to cut the apron strings and becomes more independent. He will test out his status to find out who is the pack leader: him or you. Bad habits, such as play biting, which may have been seen as endearing a few weeks earlier, should be firmly discouraged. Remember to use positive, reward-based training, but make sure your puppy knows that you are the leader and must be respected.

SECOND FEAR-IMPRINT PERIOD (6 to 14 months)

This period is not as critical as the first fear-imprint period, but it should still be handled carefully. During this time your Chihuahua may appear apprehensive, or he may show fear of something familiar. You may feel as if you have taken a backwards step, but if you adopt a calm, positive manner, your Chihuahua will see that there is nothing to be frightened of. Do not make your dog confront the thing that frightens him. Simply distract his attention and give him something else to think about, such as obeying a simple command, such as "Sit" or "Down". This will give you the opportunity to praise and reward your dog and will help to boost his confidence.

A well-socialised Chihuahua will react calmly and confidently in all situations.

YOUNG ADULTHOOD AND MATURITY (1 to 4 years)

The timing of this phase depends on the size of the dog: the bigger the dog, the later it is – so for a Chihuahua you can look for it at the beginning of this period. It coincides with a dog's physical and mental maturity. Some dogs, particularly those with a dominant nature, will test your leadership again and may become aggressive towards other dogs. Firmness and continued training are essential at this time, so that your Chihuahua accepts his status in the family pack.

IDEAS FOR SOCIALISATION

When you are socialising your Chihuahua, you want him to experience as many different situations as possible. Try out some of the following ideas, which will ensure your Chihuahua has an all-round education.

If you are taking on a rescued dog and have little knowledge of his background, it is important to work through a programme of socialisation. A young puppy soaks up new experiences like a sponge, but an older dog can still learn. If a rescued dog shows fear or apprehension, treat him in exactly the same way as you would treat a youngster who is going through the second fear-imprint period.

- Accustom your puppy to household noises, such as the vacuum cleaner, the television and the washing machine.
- Ask visitors to come to the door, wearing different types of clothing – for example, wearing a hat, a long raincoat, or carrying a stick or an umbrella.
- If you do not have children at home, make sure your Chihuahua has a chance to meet and play with them. Go to a local park and watch children in the play area. You will not be able to take your Chihuahua inside the play area, but he will see children playing and will get used to their shouts of excitement.
- Attend puppy classes. These are designed for puppies between the ages of 12 to 20 weeks and give puppies a

chance to play and interact together in a controlled, supervised environment. Your vet will have details of a local class.

- Take a walk around some quiet streets, such as a residential area, so your Chihuahua can get used to the sound of traffic. As he becomes more confident, progress to busier areas – but make sure you progress slowly, ensuring your Chihuahua is happy and confident before trying more challenging situations. Resist the temptation to pick up your Chihuahua if you think he is worried. This teaches your Chihuahua to rely on you rather than standing on his own four feet. Adopt a calm, no-nonsense manner, treating your Chihuahua like a sensible little dog, and he will gain confidence from you.

- Go to a railway station. You don't have to get on a train if you don't need to, but your Chihuahua will have the chance to experience trains, people wheeling luggage, loudspeaker announcements and going up and down stairs and over railway bridges.

- If you live in the town, plan a trip to the country. You can enjoy a day out and provide an opportunity for your Chihuahua to see livestock, such as sheep, cattle and horses.

- One of the best places for socialising a dog is at a country fair. There will be crowds of people, livestock in pens, tractors, bouncy castles, fairground rides and food stalls.

You may be thinking that all this is too much for a little Chihuahua to cope with, but if you progress slowly, giving your dog confidence when required, he will develop into a well-rounded individual. The big advantage of having a small dog is that it is easy to take him out with you. If you have a well-trained, well-socialised dog, these outings will be a great source of pleasure for you both.

TRAINING CLUBS

There are lots of training clubs to choose from, but you need to be especially careful when choosing a suitable club for a Chihuahua. If you go to a badly run club where boisterous puppies are not properly supervised, you will do more harm than good. It is important that all interactions with other dogs are a positive experience for your Chihuahua.

You can ask your vet, who will know of training clubs in your area, or you can do some research on the internet. If your Chihuahua's breeder lives locally, they may be able to help. Before you take your dog, ask if you can go to a class as an observer and find out the following:

- What experience does the instructor(s) have?
- Do they have experience with Chihuahuas?
- Is the class well organised and are the dogs reasonably quiet? (A noisy class indicates an unruly atmosphere, which will not be conducive to learning.)
- Are there are a number of classes to suit dogs of different ages and abilities?
- Are positive, reward-based training methods used?
- Does the club train for the Good Citizen Scheme (see page 102)?

If you are not happy with the training club, find another one. An inexperienced instructor who cannot handle a number of dogs in a confined environment can do more harm than good.

You may notice behavioural changes when your Chi hits adolescence.

THE ADOLESCENT CHIHUAHUA

It happens to every dog – and every owner. One minute you have an obedient well-behaved youngster and the next you have an adolescent who appears to have forgotten everything he ever learnt. Do not fall into the trap of thinking that teenage problems will only affect big dogs – a Chihuahua is just as likely to test the boundaries as he reaches maturity.

A Chihuahua male will show adolescent behaviour at any time between 12-18 months. In terms of behavioural changes, he may start to mark his territory – which is not what you want in the house! If you decide to have your Chihuahua male neutered, 18 months is probably the optimum time. Be aware that his coat will grow thicker after neutering, and he may have a tendency to put on weight. Female Chihuahuas may have a first season at around eight or nine months, but some may be as late as 14-15 months. You may even miss the first season, as a Chihuahua will keep herself very clean. Do be careful to keep a female well protected from entire males at this time, as a mating can be as quick as a flash.

Adolescence can be a trying time, but it is important to retain a sense of perspective. Look at situations from the dog's perspective and respond to uncharacteristic behaviour with firmness and consistency. Just like a teenager, an adolescent Chihuahua feels the need to challenge the status quo. But if you show that you are a strong leader (see page 80) and are quick to reward good behaviour, your Chihuahua will be happy to accept you as his protector and provider.

WHEN THINGS GO WRONG

Positive, reward-based training has proved to be the most effective method of teaching dogs, but what happens when your Chihuahua does something wrong and you need to show him that his behaviour is unacceptable? The old-fashioned school of dog training used to rely on the powers of punishment and negative reinforcement. A dog who raided the bin, for example, was smacked. Now we have learnt that it is not only unpleasant and cruel to hit a dog, it is also ineffective. If you hit a dog for stealing, he is more than likely to see you as the bad consequence of stealing, so he may raid the bin again, but probably not when you are around. If he raided the bin some time before you discovered it, he will be even more confused by your punishment, as he will not relate your response to his 'crime'.

A more commonplace example is when a dog fails to respond to a recall in the park. When the dog eventually comes back, the owner puts the dog on the lead and goes straight home to punish the dog for his poor response. Unfortunately, the dog will have a different interpretation. He does not think: "I won't ignore a recall command because the bad consequence is the end of my play in the park." He thinks: "Coming to my owner resulted in the end of playtime – therefore coming to my owner has a bad consequence, so I won't do that again."

There are a number of strategies to tackle undesirable behaviour – and they have nothing to do with harsh handling.

Ignoring bad behaviour: The Chihuahua is a clever dog who can be manipulative if you lack firmness or you are inconsistent in enforcing house rules. For example, a young Chihuahua that barks when you are preparing his food is showing his impatience and is attempting to train you, rather than the other way round. He believes he can change a situation simply by making a noise – and even if he does not get his food any quicker, he is enjoying the attention he is getting when you shout at him to tell him to be quiet. He is still getting attention, so why inhibit his behaviour?

In this situation, the best and most effective response is to ignore your Chihuahua. Suspend food preparations and get on

Jumping up and barking are both attention-seeking devices.

with another task, such as washing up. Do not go near the food or the food bowl again until your Chihuahua is calm and quiet. Repeat this on every occasion when your Chihuahua barks and he will soon learn that barking is non-productive. He is not rewarded with your attention – or with getting food. It will not take long for him to realise that being quiet is the most effective strategy. In this scenario, you have not only taught your Chihuahua to be quiet when you are preparing his food, you have also earned his respect because you have taken control of the situation.

Stopping bad behaviour: There are occasions when you want to call an instant halt to whatever it is your Chihuahua is doing. He may have just jumped on the sofa, or you may have caught him red-handed in the rubbish bin.

He has already committed the 'crime', so your aim is to stop him and to redirect his attention. You can do this by using a deep, firm tone of voice to say "No", which will startle him, and then call him to you in a bright, happy voice. If necessary, you can attract him with a toy or a treat. The moment your Chihuahua stops the undesirable behaviour and comes towards you, you can reward his good behaviour. You can back this up by running through a couple of simple exercises, such as a 'Sit' or a 'Down' and rewarding with treats. In this way, your Chihuahua focuses his attention on you and sees you as the greatest source of reward and pleasure.

In a more extreme situation, when you want to interrupt undesirable behaviour and you know that a simple "No" will not do the trick, you can try something a little more dramatic. If you get a can and fill it with pebbles, it will make a really loud noise when you shake it or throw it. The same effect can be achieved with purpose-made training discs. The dog will be startled and stop what he is doing. Even better, the dog will

Despite your best endeavours, you may encounter behavioural problems.

not associate the unpleasant noise with you. This gives you the perfect opportunity to be the nice guy, calling the dog to you and giving him lots of praise.

PROBLEM BEHAVIOUR

If you have trained your Chihuahua from puppyhood, survived his adolescence and established yourself as a fair and consistent leader, you will end up with a brilliant companion dog. The Chihuahua is a well-balanced dog, who rarely has hang-ups if he has been correctly reared and socialised. The most common cause of problem behaviour among Chihuahuas is their owners! If you treat your Chihuahua like a dog, spend time with him, and give him mental

stimulation, he will be happy and contented. If you are over-indulgent and pamper him, he will become increasingly difficult to live with, as he will not accept his place in the family pack.

It may be that you have taken on a rescued Chihuahua that has established behavioural problems. If you are worried about your Chihuahua and feel out of your depth, do not delay in seeking professional help. This is readily available, usually through a referral from your vet, or you can find out additional information on the internet (see Appendices for web addresses). An animal behaviourist will have experience in tackling problem behaviour and will be able to help both you and your dog.

RESOURCE GUARDING

If you have trained and socialised your Chihuahua correctly, he will know his place in the family pack and will have no desire to challenge your authority. As we have seen, adolescent males may test the boundaries, but this behaviour will not continue if you exhibit the necessary leadership skills.

If you have taken on a rescued dog who has not been trained and socialised, or if you have let your adolescent Chihuahua become over-assertive, you may find you have problems with a dog that is trying to get the upper hand.

Dominance is expressed in many different ways, which may include the following:
• Attention seeking – your

Chihuahua will constantly jump up at you and bark, demanding attention whenever he wants it.

- Ignoring basic obedience commands.
- Showing no respect to younger members of the family.
- Male dogs may start marking (cocking their leg) in the house.
- Aggression towards people or other dogs (see page 101).

However, the most common behaviour displayed by a Chihuahua who has ideas above his station is resource guarding. This may take a number of different forms:

- Getting up on to the sofa or your favourite armchair and growling when you tell him to get back on the floor.
- Becoming possessive over a toy, or guarding his food bowl by growling when you get too close.
- Growling when anyone approaches his bed or when anyone gets too close to where he is lying.

In each of these scenarios, the Chihuahua has something he values and he aims to keep it. He does not have sufficient respect for you, his human leader, to give up what he wants and he is 'warning' you to keep away.

If you see signs of your Chihuahua behaving in this way, you must work at lowering his status so that he realises that you are the leader and he must accept your authority. Although you

need to be firm, you also need to use positive training methods so that your Chihuahua is rewarded for the behaviour you want. In this way, his 'correct' behaviour will be strengthened and repeated.

The golden rule is not to become confrontational. The dog will see this as a challenge and may become even more determined not to co-operate. There are a number of steps you can take to lower your Chihuahua's status, which are far more likely to have a successful outcome. They include:

- Go back to basics and hold daily training sessions. Make sure you have some really tasty treats, or find a toy your Chihuahua really values and only bring it out at training sessions. Run through all the training exercises you have taught your Chihuahua. Remember, boredom is very often the key to undesirable behaviour. By giving him things to do, you are giving him mental stimulation and you have the opportunity to make a big fuss of him and reward him when he does well. This will help to reinforce the message that you are the leader and that it is rewarding to do as you ask.
- Teach your Chihuahua something new; this can be as simple as learning a trick, such as begging for a treat. Having something new to think about will mentally stimulate your

Chihuahua and he will benefit from interacting with you.

- Be 100 per cent consistent with all house rules – your Chihuahua must never sit on the sofa unless he is invited, and he should always be ignored if he barks to get your attention.
- If your Chihuahua is becoming possessive over toys, remove all his toys and keep them out of reach. It is then up to you to decide when to produce a toy and to initiate a game. Equally, it is you who will decide when the game is over and when to

A Chi may become possessive over a toy and refuse to give it up on request.

Resource guarding shows that a dog does not accept his position in the family pack and is seeking to better it.

remove the toy. This teaches your Chihuahua that you 'own' his toys. He has fun playing and interacting with you, but the game is over – and the toy is given up – when you say so.

- If your Chihuahua has been guarding his food bowl, put the bowl down empty and drop in food a little at a time. Periodically stop dropping in the food and tell your Chihuahua "Sit" and "Wait". Give it a few seconds and then reward him by dropping in more food. This shows your Chihuahua that you are the provider of the food and he can only eat when you allow him to.

- Make sure the family eats before you feed your Chihuahua. Some trainers advocate eating in front of the dog (maybe just a few bites from a biscuit) before starting a training session, so the dog appreciates your elevated status.

SEPARATION ANXIETY
A Chihuahua should be brought up to accept short periods of separation from his owner so that he does not become anxious. A new puppy should be left for short periods on his own, ideally in a crate where he cannot get up to any mischief. It is a good idea to leave him with a boredom-busting toy so he will be happily occupied in your absence. When you return, do not rush to the crate and make a huge fuss. Wait a few minutes, and then calmly go to the crate and release your dog, telling him how good he has been. If this scenario is repeated a number of times, your Chihuahua will soon learn that being left on his own is no big deal.

Problems with separation anxiety are most likely to arise if you take on a rescued dog who has major insecurities. You may also find that your Chihuahua hates being left if you have failed to accustom him to short periods of isolation when he was growing up. Separation anxiety is expressed in a number of ways and all are equally distressing for both dog and owner. An anxious dog who is left alone may bark and whine continuously, urinate and defecate, and may be extremely destructive.

There are a number of steps you can take when attempting to solve this problem:
- Put up a baby-gate between adjoining rooms and leave your dog in one room while you are in the other room. Your dog will be able to see you and hear you, but he is learning to cope without being right next to you. Build up the amount of time you can leave your dog in easy stages.
- Buy some boredom-busting toys and fill them with some tasty treats. Whenever you leave your dog, give him a food-filled toy so that he is busy while you are away.
- If you have not used a crate before, it is not too late to start. Make sure the crate is cosy and train your Chihuahua to get used to going in his crate while

A kong stuffed with food will give your Chihuahua an occupation while you are away.

you are in the same room. Gradually build up the amount of time he spends in the crate and then start leaving the room for short periods. When you return, do not make a fuss of your dog. Leave him for five or ten minutes before releasing him, so that he gets used to your comings and goings.

• Pretend to go out, putting on your coat and jangling keys, but do not leave the house. An anxious dog often becomes hyped up by the ritual of leaving and this will help to desensitize him.

• When you go out, leave a radio or a TV on. Some dogs are comforted by hearing voices and background noise when they are left alone.

• Try to make your absences as short as possible when you are first training your Chi to accept being on his own.

If you take these steps, your dog should become less anxious and, over a period of time, you should be able to solve the problem. However, if you are failing to make progress, do not delay in calling in expert help.

AGGRESSION

Aggression is a complex issue, as there are different causes and the behaviour may be triggered by numerous factors. It may be directed towards people, but far more commonly it is directed towards other dogs. Aggression in dogs may be the result of:

• Assertive behaviour (see page 98).

• Defensive behaviour: This may be induced by fear, pain or punishment.

• Territory: A dog may become aggressive if strange dogs or people enter his territory (which is generally seen as the house and garden).

• Intra-sexual issues: This is aggression between sexes – male-to-male or female-to-female.

• Parental instinct: A mother dog may become aggressive if she is protecting her puppies.

It is very rare for the Chihuahua to show signs of aggression. It is not in the nature of the breed, and if it does occur, it is the result of bad experiences or inappropriate handling. It is essential that resource guarding is nipped in the bud so that a Chihuahua does not try to challenge his owner. Equally, all interactions with other dogs must be controlled and supervised so a Chihuahua does not become fearful and defensive.

However, if you are concerned about your dog's behaviour, you would be well advised to call in professional help. If the aggression is directed towards people, you should seek immediate advice. This behaviour can escalate very quickly and could lead to disastrous consequences.

NEW CHALLENGES
If you enjoy training your Chihuahua, you may want to try one of the many dog sports that are now on offer.

GOOD CITIZEN SCHEME
This is a scheme run by the Kennel Club in the UK and the American Kennel Club in the USA. The schemes promote responsible ownership and help you to train a well-behaved dog who will fit in with the community. The schemes are excellent for all pet owners and will give your Chihuahua the opportunity to meet other dogs

The clever Chihuahua will enjoy the challenge of more advanced training. This is Culcia Pixie's Gift (Danny) who won his gold award in the Good Citizen Scheme.

in a controlled situation. The KC and the AKC schemes vary in format. In the UK there are three levels: bronze, silver and gold, with each test becoming progressively more demanding. However, the tests are well within the capabilities of a well-trained Chihuahua. In the AKC scheme there is a single test.

Some of the exercises include:

• Walking on a loose lead among people and other dogs.
• Recall amid distractions.
• A controlled greeting where dogs stay under control while their owners meet.
• The dog allows all-over grooming and handling by his owner, and also accepts being handled by the examiner.
• Stays, with the owner in sight and then out of sight.
• Food manners, allowing the owner to eat without begging and taking a treat on command.
• Sendaway – sending the dog to his bed.

The tests are designed to show the control you have over your dog and his ability to respond correctly and remain calm in all situations. The Good Citizen Scheme is taught at most training clubs. For more information, log on to the Kennel Club or AKC website (see Appendices).

You need a top-quality Chihuahua to compete in the show ring.

SHOWING

In your eyes, your Chihuahua is the most beautiful dog in the world – but would a judge agree? Showing is a highly competitive sport at the top level, and it can be demanding in terms of both time and money. However, many owners get bitten by the showing bug, and their calendar is governed by the dates of the top showing fixtures.

To be successful in the show ring, a Chihuahua must conform as closely as possible to the Breed Standard, which is a written blueprint describing the 'perfect' Chi (see Chapter Seven). To get started you need to buy a puppy that has show potential and then train him to perform in the ring. A Chihuahua will be expected to stand in show pose, gait for the judge in order to show off his natural movement, and be examined by the judge. This involves a detailed hands-on examination, so your Chihuahua must be bombproof when handled by strangers.

Many training clubs hold ringcraft classes, which are run by experienced showgoers. At these classes, you will learn how to handle your Chihuahua in the ring, and you will also find out about rules, procedures and show-ring etiquette.

The best plan is to start off at some small, informal shows where you can practise and learn the tricks of the trade before graduating to bigger shows. It's a long haul starting in the very first puppy class, but the dream is to make your Chihuahua a Champion.

COMPETITIVE OBEDIENCE

In the UK, the sport of competitive obedience is dominated by Border Collies, Working Sheepdogs, German

A Chi can be trained to a surprisingly high level in competitive obedience.

Beginners, but this is highly competitive, even at the lower levels. Marks are lost for even the slightest crooked angle noticed when the dog is sitting and if a dog has a momentary attention deficit or works too far away from his owner in heelwork, again points will be deducted. Competition is open to dogs from the age of six months. The exercises include the following:

• **Heelwork:** Dog and handler must complete a set pattern on and off the lead, which includes left turns, right turns, about turns and changes of pace.

• **Recall:** This may be when the handler is stationary or on the move.

• **Retrieve:** This may be a dumbbell or any article chosen by the judge.

• **Sendaway:** The dog is sent to a designated spot and must go into an instant 'Down' until he is recalled by the handler.

• **Stays:** The dog must stay in the 'Sit' and in the 'Down' for a set amount of time. In advanced classes, the handler is out of sight.

• **Scent:** The dog must retrieve a single cloth from a pre-arranged pattern of cloths that has his owner's scent or, in advanced classes, the judge's scent. There may also be decoy cloths.

• **Distance control.** The dog must execute a series of moves ('Sit', 'Stand', 'Down') without moving from his position and with the handler at a distance.

Shepherds, Belgian Shepherds, and some of the gundog breeds. However in the US, a wide variety of breeds take part – including Toy dogs – and many do very well. The Chihuahua is a clever, quick-thinking little dog, and if you have the patience, there is no reason why your dog should not be able to master the exercises. There are various levels of achievement, starting with

Even though competitive obedience requires accuracy and precision, make sure you make it fun for your Chihuahua, with lots of praise and rewards so that you motivate him to do his best. Many training clubs run advanced classes for those who want to compete in obedience, or you can hire the services of a professional trainer for one-on-one sessions.

AGILITY

This fun sport has grown enormously in popularity over the past few years, and both Chihuahuas and Chihuahua crosses have competed with some success, particularly in the US.

In agility competitions, each dog must complete a set course over a series of obstacles. For small dogs, the hurdles, long jump and tyre are set at a reduced height – all the other equipment is the same for all sizes. It includes:
• Jumps (upright hurdles and long jump)
• Weaves
• A-frame
• Dog walk
• Seesaw
• Tunnels (collapsible and rigid)
• Tyre

Dogs may compete in Jumping classes, with jumps, tunnels and weaves, or in Agility classes, which have the full set of equipment. Faults are awarded

DANCING WITH DOGS

This sport is relatively new, but it is becoming increasingly popular. It is very entertaining to watch, but it is certainly not as simple as it looks. To perform a choreographed routine to music with your Chihuahua demands a huge amount of training.

Dancing with dogs is divided into two categories: heelwork to music and canine freestyle. In heelwork to music, the dog must work closely with his handler and show a variety of close 'heelwork' positions. In canine freestyle, the routine can be more flamboyant, with the dog working at a distance from the handler and performing spectacular tricks. Routines are judged on style and presentation, content and accuracy.

for poles down on the jumps, missed contact points on the A-frame, dog walk and seesaw, and refusals. If a dog takes the wrong course, he is eliminated. The winner is the dog that completes the course in the fastest time with no faults. As you move up the levels, courses become progressively harder with more twists, turns and changes of direction.

If you want to get involved in agility, you will need to find a club that specialises in the sport (see Appendices). You will not be allowed to start training until your Chihuahua is 12 months old and you cannot compete

until he is 18 months old. This rule is for the protection of the dog, who may suffer injury if he puts strain on bones and joints while he is still growing.

SUMMING UP

The Chihuahua is an outstanding companion dog – and once you have owned one, no other breed will do. He is intelligent, loving and loyal. Make sure you keep your half of the bargain: spend time socialising and training your Chihuahua so that you can be proud to take him anywhere and he will always be a credit to you.

THE PERFECT CHIHUAHUA

Chapter 7

When you bought your Chihuahua, you probably never thought that you would be interested in showing. However, when you own a pedigree dog, you may well become interested in the breed and wonder why some dogs become Champions but others fail to make the grade. Newcomers to the show ring imagine the judge looks at a line-up of dogs in the ring and then decides which dog they like best. This has an element of truth. The judge is making a personal choice, but his or her decision is governed by the stipulations of the Breed Standard. This is a written blueprint of how the breed should be in terms of appearance, movement and temperament. It is the dog that, in the judge's opinion, most closely matches the Breed

Standard that will be the one that wins.

If you have a top-quality dog, it is great to receive honours and admiration, but there is a more serious side to showing. If pedigree dogs were produced without judging them against the Breed Standard, it would not be long before you would see a variety of types. Dogs might get bigger or smaller; they might have small ears or lack the distinctive Chihuahua movement. Soon the grade that was developed hundreds of years ago would be lost in a hotchpotch of small, indistinguishable dogs. If we are to preserve the Chihuahua, we must produce dogs that conform as closely as possible to the Breed Standard. The dogs that win in the ring carry a great responsibility because they will be the animals that are used for breeding. It is vitally important that they carry

the true characteristics of the breed and are sound in mind and body.

AIMING FOR PERFECTION

The aim of the breeder is to produce a litter of fit, healthy puppies and in the hope that one or two individuals may have the quality to compete in the show ring. This may sound not too difficult, but I can assure you that it is far from easy. You would think that if you mated a top-quality male with a top-quality female, you would be guaranteed success – but it does not work out like that. When you are matching a male and a female, you need to consider what they look like, what their temperament is like, and whether they are sound and healthy. But there is more to it than this. Each dog is the product of generations of breeding and may carry characteristics of ancestors that

A bitch that is used for breeding must be big enough to carry her puppies through pregnancy and be able to whelp them successfully.

go back many years. So the skilful breeder has to refer to the bloodlines of both dog and bitch to be sure there are no outstanding faults running through either family. This should include a thorough investigation into health records. There are some inherited conditions in the breed and it is essential that these be eliminated from any breeding programme.

You need to use a brood bitch that it physically capable of carrying puppies. This can obviously be a problem for a tiny animal. Generally, the bitch should weigh a minimum of 4 lbs (1.8 kgs); she should have a wide pelvis and not be too narrow at the back end. It is important to

find out whether females in the line are self-whelpers and can deliver puppies without needing a Caesarean. If the female needs a Caesarean, it is highly likely that her daughter will also have whelping difficulties. I would not knowingly breed from a bitch that might need a Caesarean or has a history of Caesareans in her background. Obviously, puppies can be successfully reared after a Caesar, but the mother is at considerable risk. Chihuahuas respond badly to anaesthetic and a tiny dog is very difficult to anaesthetise. It is a procedure that should only be undertaken when strictly necessary.

Now comes the most difficult part. The breeder has discarded

the dogs that clearly have faults – they have probably gone to lovely homes – but what about producing puppies that are as good as their parents or, perhaps, even better? The aim is to find a male and female that complement each other, cementing the good points and improving minor faults. For example, if a female did not have the best ear carriage, you would look for a male that is strong in this department, and you really do need to look back in the pedigree and see what the antecedents have done.

Generally, there are three types of breeding programmes used in the dog world:
• **In-breeding**: This involves

Every breeder dreams that their promising puppy will mature into a Champion.

breeding two very closely related dogs. The Kennel Club does not allow too much close breeding. You cannot register father-to-daughter or mother-to-son matings. This type of breeding tends to exaggerate faults in the line and there is an increased risk of inherited disorders. It should only be attempted by a very experienced breeder who knows the dogs that are involved.

- **Out-crossing**: This is the mating of two totally unrelated dogs, which have no relatives in common. It is a method of introducing new blood to a line, and if you produce the result you are hoping for, you can go on to fix a type by line-breeding. In fact, probably far back in the pedigree there will be common ancestry.

- **Line-breeding**: This is similar to in-breeding. It involves members of the same family but they are not so closely related. This is the most commonly used breeding programme, as it retains the virtues of the line but also introduces new blood into a kennel.

EVALUATING PUPPIES

Breeders throughout history have been trying to produce the perfect puppy, but, unfortunately, there is no such thing as certainty when you are breeding pedigree dogs. To the layperson, a litter of Chihuahua puppies looks irresistible but it takes years of experience to spot a Champion in the making. Some breeders claim they can tell if a puppy is of show quality almost from the moment it is born. Others prefer to wait a little longer before making a choice. In fact, it is nearly impossible to decide. Perhaps, just occasionally, you will get a feeling – but all you can do is use your experience, and hope! It easier to pick out a possible future winner with smoothcoats; longcoat puppies seem to change more as they grow up. So, your gorgeous puppies in the nest may grow up to be swans or maybe they will be ugly ducklings – but they are all adorable.

The basic structure of the head and skull will alter very little. By the time the pup is two weeks old, the typical apple-dome should be apparent. The puppy should have large, dark eyes and big ears, although at this age the puppy's ears may not be erect. Sometimes they become erect when the puppy is eight weeks old, sometimes they take longer. If you have an otherwise beautiful puppy with slightly soft ears, it is worth persevering because they may well come up by the time your pup is old enough to show at six months of age. If, sadly, the ears are still soft and do not want to come up, you have still got a beautiful puppy to sell to somebody.

Because the Chihuahua is known as a 'head breed', the apple-dome, large, lustrous eyes and big ears are typical of the breed – but you need more than a good head. You need every feature to conform as closely as possible to the Breed Standard, but, in the show ring, the Chihuahua must have a good head to be successful. Most breeders will wait until the litter is eight weeks old before making a final evaluation. I think this is probably much too early because the puppies will continue to change. At eight weeks the pups will be on their feet and moving. You will be able to assess temperament – who is introverted and who is extroverted? But you should not

Despite its small size, a puppy should look sturdy and balanced.

be selling your puppies until they are at least 12 weeks, so do not worry if, at eight weeks, you really cannot decide. If you have several promising puppies, adhering closely to the Standard, you may have to run them on for several months. Chihuahua puppies do not cost very much to keep, so it will pay you to do this.

The pup with show potential should look strong, sturdy and balanced. The body should be compact and he should not be too long in the leg. Although the

Chihuahua is a tiny dog, he should be completely in proportion. A good rule is to look at your Chihuahua and say: if this were a big dog, would it be balanced and in proportion? If the answer is no, then your Chihuahua is not of show quality. Generally, longcoated Chihuahuas go through more changes than the smoothcoats. In fact, my experience is that a smoothcoated male will not change very much. If he goes off a little bit as a junior, he will come back. It is unlikely that he will go off completely.

In both longcoats and smoothcoats, you must have a Chihuahua with ring presence. This is the dog that says, "Look at me! Don't bother to look at anyone else." A dog that has natural showmanship is highly valued.

THE BREED STANDARDS
The Breed Standard is drawn up under the auspices of the national kennel club, and there may be minor differences in the Standard depending on where you live. For the purposes of analysis and interpretation, we have reproduced the Kennel Club (KC) Breed Standard, which is used in the UK, the American Kennel Club (AKC) Breed Standard, which us used in the USA, and the Federation Cynologique Internationale (FCI) Standard, which covers Europe and the rest of the world.

In the UK, all Breed Standards are prefaced with the following:

A Breed Standard is the guideline which describes the ideal characteristics, temperament and appearance of a breed, but it also ensures that the breed is fit for function. Absolute soundness is essential. Breeders and judges should at all times be careful to avoid obvious conditions or exaggerations which would be detrimental in any way to the health, welfare or soundness of this breed. From time to time certain conditions or exaggerations may be considered to have the potential to affect dogs in some breeds adversely; judges and breeders are requested to refer to the Kennel Club website for details of any such current issues. If a feature or quality is desirable, it should only be present in the right measure.

ANALYSING THE BREED STANDARD

GENERAL APPEARANCE/ CHARACTERISTICS
KC
Small, dainty, compact. Characteristics: Alert little dog; swift-moving with brisk, forceful action and saucy expression.

AKC
A graceful, alert, swift-moving compact little dog with saucy expression, and with terrier-like qualities of temperament. Proportions: The body is off-square; hence, slightly longer when measured from point of shoulder to point of buttocks, than height at the withers. Somewhat shorter bodies are preferred in males.

FCI
This dog has a compact body. Of great importance is the fact that his skull is apple-shaped and that he carries his moderately long tail very high, either curved or forming the shape of a semicircle with the tip pointing towards the loin region.
Important proportions: Length of body slightly greater than height at withers. Desired, however, is an almost square body, especially in males. In bitches, because of the function of reproduction, a slightly longer body is permitted.

In the Kennel Club Breed Standard, the Chihuahua is described as small, dainty and compact, and is noted for his saucy expression. This latter characteristic is open to interpretation, but a bold, slightly impudent expression is very typical of the Chihuahua's outlook on life.

From an early age, the typical apple dome skull and large, lustrous eyes are apparent.

Ch. Dachida's Johnnie Angel: A fine representative from the UK's leading smoothcoat kennel.

Am. Ch. Ouachitah For Your Eyes Only: The only Chihuahua to win the Toy Group at Westminster. *Photo: Gilbert Photography.*

TEMPERAMENT

KC

Gay, spirited and intelligent, neither snappy nor withdrawn.

AKC

Alert, projecting the 'terrier-like' attitudes of self importance, confidence, self-reliance.

FCI

Quick, alert, lively and very courageous.

Temperament is so, so important. A Chihuahua should never be bad tempered or snappy. After all, if it were a bigger dog, you would not put up with it – the dog would be dangerous. Sadly, some Chihuahuas do not have very good temperaments. Hopefully, now with the slightly revised Kennel Club Standard, a bad temperament will be penalised. It is just not acceptable to have a snappy, bad-tempered Chihuahua. A little bit of bounce, standoffishness, and showmanship is important if you are showing your dog. But the most important thing is that your dog should be friendly, affectionate and loving – not only to you, but to those he meets.

The Chihuahua is small, dainty and compact with a saucy expression.

HEAD AND SKULL

KC

Well rounded 'apple dome' skull, cheeks and jaws lean, muzzle moderately short, slightly pointed. Definite stop.

AKC

A well rounded "apple dome" skull, with or without molera. Stop: Well defined. When viewed in profile, it forms a near 90 degree angle where muzzle joins skull.
Muzzle: Moderately short, slightly pointed. Cheeks and jaws lean.
Nose: Self-colored in blond types, or black. In moles, blues, and chocolates, they are self-colored. In blond types, pink noses permissible.

FCI

CRANIAL REGION:
Skull: Well rounded apple head (a characteristic of the breed) preferably without a fontanel although a small one is allowed. Stop: Well marked, deep and broad as the forehead is bulging over the set-on of muzzle.
FACIAL REGION:
Nose: Any colour permitted. Moderately short, pointing

113

The skull is well rounded, and the muzzle is moderately short.

Viewed in profile, the stop – where the muzzle goes to the skull – is well defined.

slightly upwards.
Muzzle: Short, straight seen from side, broad at set-on, tapering towards the tip.
Lips: Lean and close fitting.
Cheeks: Only slightly developed, very clean.

Typically, the Chihuahua should have a well-rounded skull, which is described as an "apple-dome". This just means that it is fairly rounded. The cheeks and the jaw should be lean. The muzzle should not be long nor should it be too short, it should be slightly pointed. The stop, where the muzzle goes to the skull, should be well defined.

In the early days of the breed, the molera (where the skull plates do not close completely) was a distinguishing feature. Judges used to feel for the small opening on the top of the skull as it was considered a desirable trait. This is no longer the case; it is now considered that a molera leaves the head and brain too vulnerable if the dog hits his head.

I would hope and expect all skull plates to have closed by the time a dog was exhibited in the ring – at approximately six months – but is not unusual to find a molera in a young puppy. Occasionally the plates do not close as the dog matures, but I would consider this undesirable and would not use such a dog for breeding.

EYES
KC
Large, round, but not protruding; set well apart; centre of eye is on a plane with lowest point of ear and base of stop; dark or ruby. Light eyes in light colours permissible.

AKC
Expression: Saucy.
Eyes: Full, round, but not protruding, balanced, set well apart-luminous dark or luminous ruby. Light eyes in blond or white-colored dogs permissible. Blue eyes or a difference in the color of the iris in the two eyes, or two different colors within one iris should be considered a serious fault.

FCI
Large, roundish in shape, very expressive, not protruding, perfectly dark. Light eyes permissible, but not desired.

The centre of the eye is on a plane with the lowest point of the ear and base at the stop. They should be dark or ruby. Light eyes in light colours are permissible but they are not so well favoured. It was not uncommon to see ruby eyes in cream dogs, but it has become much rarer. This is probably because a lot of judges did not like the lighter eye and because those dogs did not win, people did not breed them.

EARS
KC
Large, flaring, set on at an angle of approximately 45 degrees; giving breadth between ears. Tipped or broken down highly undesirable.

AKC
Large, erect type ears, held more upright when alert, but flaring to the sides at a 45 degree angle when in repose, giving breadth between the ears. Disqualifications: Broken down or cropped ears.

FCI
Large, upright, widely open, broad at set-on, gradually tapering towards their slightly rounded point. In repose inclined laterally forming an angle of 45 degrees.

The ears are an important feature of the breed. They are large and flaring, set at an angle of approximately 45 degrees, giving breadth between the ears. Pricked

The ears are large and held more upright when the dog is alert. This is the multi Best in Show winner Ch. Bramerita Naughty But Nice.

Photo: Carol Ann Johnson.

or broken down ears are highly undesirable. This is not important in a pet, but it is no use to try to show a dog with soft ears. A Chihuahua's ears must be strong and flared, not pointed at the tip but well rounded.

MOUTH
KC
Jaws strong, with a perfect, regular and complete scissor bite, i.e. upper teeth closely overlapping lower teeth and set square to the jaws.

AKC
Bite: Level or scissors. Overshot or undershot, or any

The jaws are strong with a scissor bite, the upper teeth closely overlapping the lower teeth.

The forequarters are strong with a well-developed chest.

distortion of the bite or jaw, should be penalized as a serious fault. A missing tooth or two is permissible.

FCI
Scissor or pincer bite. Overshot, undershot, as well as any other anomaly in position of upper or lower jaw must be strictly penalized.

The jaw should be strong with a perfect, regular, complete scissor bite. An undershot mouth is not desirable but, again, if your Chihuahua is a pet, it is of no major significance. A wry mouth, which is where the jaw does not meet properly and is not properly aligned, is definitely not desirable, but still these dogs can make lovely pets.

NECK
KC
Slightly arched, medium length.
AKC
Slightly arched, gracefully sloping into lean shoulders.

FCI
Upper profile slightly arched.
Length: Medium length.
Shape: Thicker in dogs than in bitches.
Skin: Without dewlap. In the long-haired variety, the presence of a neck-ruff with longer hair is highly desirable.

The neck should be slightly arched, of medium length and sloping into lean shoulders. It is quite important that the neck is a reasonable length; it does set the dog off and make him look better. Very short necks are not desirable. If the head looks as if it

comes more or less straight on to the shoulders, again, this is not desirable. It will not affect the dog in any way, but it does not look so good. A decent, 'reachy' swan neck sets off the elegance of a Chihuahua and it is much desired.

FOREQUARTERS
KC
Shoulders well laid; lean, sloping into slightly broadening support above straight forelegs, set well under chest giving freedom of movement without looseness.

AKC
Shoulders: Lean, sloping into a slightly broadening support above straight forelegs that set well under, giving free movement at the elbows.

The topline is level and the ribs well rounded.

Shoulders should be well up, giving balance and soundness, sloping into a level back (never down or low). This gives a well developed chest and strength of forequarters.

FCI
Forelegs straight and of good length; seen from the front, they form a straight line with the elbows. Seen from the side, they are upright.
Shoulders: Clean and moderately muscled. Good angulation between shoulder-blade and upper arm.
Elbows: Firm and fitting close to body which ensures free movement. Pasterns: Slightly sloping, strong and flexible.

The forequarters should slope into a slightly broadening support of the straight front legs. The front legs should be set well under the chest to give freedom of movement. When a Chihuahua moves, it is also important that the shoulders are not tight. You do not want too much width at the front.

BODY
KC
Level back. Body, from point of shoulder to rear point of croup, slightly longer than height at withers. Well sprung ribs, deep brisket.

AKC
Topline: Level. Body: Ribs rounded and well sprung (but not too much "barrel-shaped").

FCI
Compact and well built.
Topline: Level.

Withers: Only slightly marked.
Back: Short and firm.
Loin: Strongly muscled.
Croup: Broad and strong; almost flat or slightly sloping.
Chest: Ribcage broad and deep, ribs well sprung. Seen from front, roomy but not exaggerated. Seen from side, reaching to elbows. Not barrel shaped.
Lower Line: Formed by a clearly tucked up belly. Slack belly is permitted but not desired.

The body should be level, with a level back from the point of the shoulder to the rear point of the croup. The Chihuahua should be slightly longer than its height at the withers. However, it is less important to have the shorter back in a bitch. A longer back in a bitch, particularly if you are breeding from her, is not a bad

HINDQUARTERS

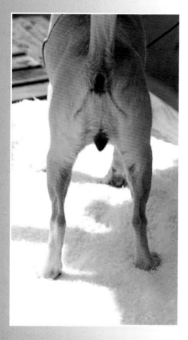

The hindquarters are muscular with hocks well apart.

idea, as it gives her more room. More important, the dog should be boxy, more or less as high as he is long. If you took a line from just below the neck to the tail set, it should be level and slightly longer, particularly in a bitch. The ribs should be well rounded but not too barrel-shaped.

HINDQUARTERS
KC
Muscular; hocks well let down, with good turn of stifle, well apart, turning neither in nor out.

AKC
Muscular, with hocks well apart, neither out nor in, well let down, firm and sturdy. Angulation: Should equal that of forequarters.

FCI
Hindlegs well muscled with long bones, vertical and parallel to each other with good angulation at hip, knee and hock joints, in harmony with angulation of forequarters.
Hocks: Short with well developed Achilles' tendons; seen from rear, they are well apart, straight and vertical.

The hocks should be muscular, well let down with a good, turned stifle; they should be set well apart, turning neither in nor out. Although the Chihuahua is such a little dog, he is well put together and well

made. This is seen particularly in the hindquarters, which should be muscular and sturdy. The hocks, which are short, should be close to the ground. Unsoundness is highly undesirable. Unfortunately, patella luxation, which means slipping knee caps where the tendon just comes out of the groove over the hock, is a definite unsoundness and you should never breed from an unsound dog of either sex.

FEET
KC
Small and dainty, turning neither in nor out; toes well divided but not spread, pads cushioned, fine, strong, flexible pasterns. Neither hare- nor cat-like, nails moderately short.

AKC
A small, dainty foot with toes well split up but not spread, pads cushioned. (Neither the hare nor the cat foot.) Dewclaws may be removed. Pasterns: Strong.

FCI
Very small and oval with toes well apart but not splayed (neither hare- nor cat-foot). Nails particularly well arched and moderately long. Pads well developed and very elastic. Pasterns: Slightly sloping, strong and flexible. Dewclaws must be removed *except in countries where this practice is forbidden by law.*

The tail carriage – which should be up and over the back – is identical in both varieties, despite the feathering that gives a different appearance.

The feet should be small and dainty, not turning in or out. The toes should be well divided, but not spread. Feet should be neither hare-like nor cat-like, with pads cushioned and nails moderately short. The Chihuahua should have fine, strong, flexible pasterns.

TAIL
KC
Medium length, set high, carried up and over back (sickle tail). When moving never tucked under or curled below the topline. Furry, flattish in appearance, broadening slightly in centre and tapering to point.

AKC
Moderately long, carried sickle either up or out, or in a loop over the back with tip just touching the back. (Never tucked between legs.) Disqualifications: Docked tail, bobtail.

The tail should be of medium length, set high, carried up and over the back most of the time. When moving, it should never touch under or be curled below the topline. It should be flat, furry in appearance, broadening slightly in the centre and tapering to a point. In fact, the flat, furry tail is very much a feature of the breed and it does set the dog off. Thin tails are not desirable, although they are still seen occasionally. But seeing a Chihuahua moving nicely with a tail carried well does set off the breed and it really is a delight to watch. If your Chihuahua is carrying his tail down, he is not very happy.

GAIT/MOVEMENT
KC
Brisk, forceful action, neither high-stepping nor hackney; good reach without slackness in forequarters, good drive in hindquarters. Viewed from front and behind legs should move neither too close nor too wide, with no turning in or out of feet or pasterns. Topline should remain firm and level when moving.

AKC
The Chihuahua should move swiftly with a firm, sturdy action, with good reach in front equal to the drive from the rear. From the rear, the hocks remain parallel to each other, and the foot fall of the rear legs follows directly behind that of the forelegs. The legs, both front

Movement should be brisk and forceful.

The drive comes from the hindquarters.

and rear, will tend to converge slightly toward a central line of gravity as speed increases. The side view shows good, strong drive in the rear and plenty of reach in the front, with head carried high. The topline should remain firm and the backline level as the dog moves.

FCI
Steps are long, springy, energetic and active with good reach and drive. Seen from rear, hind legs should move almost parallel to each other, so that the footprints of the hind feet fit directly into those of the front feet. With increasing speed, the limbs show a tendency to converge towards the centre point of gravity (single track). Movement remains free and springy

without visible effort, head raised and back firm.

The movement of a Chihuahua should be brisk, with a forceful action, neither high-stepping nor hackney. There should be good reach without slackness in the forequarters, and good drive from the hindquarters. Viewed from the front and behind, the legs should move neither too close nor too wide, with no turning in or out of the feet or pasterns. The topline should remain firm and level when the dog is moving. The brisk, forceful action is very much a Chihuahua thing – they move quickly. People think that because the Chihuahua is a Toy dog, he does not need a lot of exercise or a lot of room, but this is not so. Chihuahuas revel in exercise and when you are showing, you need a decent-size

ring so your dog can really show off his gait.

COAT
KC
Smooth Coat: Smooth, of soft texture, close and glossy, with undercoat and ruff permissible. Long Coat: Soft texture (never coarse or harsh to touch) either flat or slightly wavy. Never tight and curly. Feathering on ears, feet and legs, pants on hindquarters, large ruff on neck desirable. Tail long and full as a plume

AKC
Smooth Coat: The coat should be of soft texture, close and glossy. (Heavier coats with undercoats permissible.) Coat placed well over body with ruff on neck preferred, and more scanty on head and ears. Hair

The two varieties are identical in every detail, with the exception of the coat.

on tail preferred furry.
Long Coat: The coat should be of a soft texture, either flat or slightly wavy, with undercoat preferred. Ears: Fringed. Tail: Full and long (as a plume). Feathering on feet and legs, pants on hind legs and large ruff on the neck desired and preferred. (The Chihuahua should be groomed only to create a neat appearance.) Disqualification: In Long Coats, too thin coat that resembles bareness.

FCI
SKIN: Smooth and elastic all over body.
HAIR: In this breed there are two varieties of coat:
• Smooth-haired: Coat is short, lying close all over body. If there is an undercoat, the hair is somewhat longer; sparse coat on throat and belly permissible; slightly longer on neck and tail, short on face and ears. Coat is glossy and its texture is soft. Hairless dogs are not tolerated.
• Long-haired: Coat should be fine and silky, smooth or slightly wavy. Not too thick undercoat desired. Coat is longer, forming feathering on ears, neck, rear of front and hind legs, on feet and on tail. Dogs with long billowing coat will not be accepted.

There are two coats in Chihuahuas. The original Chihuahuas were smoothcoats, and they carry the dominant gene. Their coat should be soft in texture, glossy and close to the body. Longcoats should have coats of a soft texture, never coarse or harsh to touch. The coat can be either flat or slightly wavy, but never tight and curly. There should be feathering on the ears, feet and legs and the hindquarters. A large ruff on the neck is desirable, but you do not want too heavy a coat. The tail should be long and full as a plume.

COLOUR
KC
Any colour or mixture of colours - but never merle (dapple).

AKC
Any color - Solid, marked or splashed.

FCI
All colours in all possible shades and combinations are admitted.

All colours are permitted, but the Kennel Club excludes merles. The Kennel Club will not register merle puppies, nor will it register progeny from merle parents. This colour brings with it some very severe faults – both deafness and blindness have been found in the merle Chihuahua.

Research has found the merle gene is not found in Chihuahuas, so a merle Chihuahua cannot be a purebred specimen. Puppies also tend to be of very poor quality, and so breed specialists in the UK campaigned to have the colour excluded from the Breed Standard.

A revised Breed Standard now asks for a bigger dog.

SIZE
KC
Weight: Up to 2.7 kgs (6 lbs), with 1.8-2.7 kgs (4-6 lbs) preferred.

AKC
A well balanced little dog not to exceed 6 lbs.
Disqualification: Any dog over 6 lbs in weight.

FCI
In this breed only the weight is taken into consideration, not the height.
Weight: Ideal weight between 1.5 and 3 kg.
However, dogs between 500 gr and 1.5 kg are accepted.
Subjects weighing more than 3 kg shall be disqualified.

The Kennel Club has revised the weight and now asks for the upper end of the weight scale. Previously it stated a preference for dogs that weighed between 1-4 lbs (1-1.8 kgs), and added: "If two dogs are equally good in type, the more diminutive is preferred". The weight is now up to 2.7 kilograms (6 lbs) with 1.8-2.7 kilograms (4-6 lbs) preferred. The American Standard is clear in stating that dogs should not exceed 6 lbs (2.7 kgs).

Interestingly, the danger of producing dogs that are too small was highlighted by breed expert Hilary Harmer, writing in the 1960s, long before the current revision of the Breed Standard. When analysing the Breed Standard she writes: "Luckily, in the Chihuahua Breed Standard, there is nothing laid down that is over-exaggerated, and which could be detrimental to the breed in any way. Even the great difference in size which is permitted, that is to say two to six pounds, is perhaps the saving grace in preventing the breed from becoming too small which it so easily could do".

Over a period of time, the Chihuahua has become a slightly bigger dog and most dogs are 4 lbs or over. This is entirely for the good of the breed, as the bigger dogs seem to have fewer health problems compared with the tinies; they are definitely sounder and they do appear to live longer. The Chihuahua is not weighed at the ringside, so the judge must rely on his or her own evaluation of weight and size. Obviously it is important that the smallest breed of all does not lose its unique status, but it is equally important that the Chihuahua should be a fit and healthy breed. In fact, it is vitally important that they should be fit and healthy.

FAULTS &
DISQUALIFICATIONS
KC
Any departure from the foregoing points should be considered a fault and the seriousness with which the fault should be regarded should be in exact proportion to its degree and its effect upon the health and welfare of the dog.

Note: Male animals should have two apparently normal

testicles fully descended into the scrotum.

AKC
Any dog over 6 lbs in weight. Broken down or cropped ears. Docked tail, bobtail. In Long Coats, too thin coat that resembles bareness.

FCI
FAULTS: Any departure from the foregoing points should be considered a fault and the seriousness with which the fault should be regarded should be in exact proportion to its degree.
- Missing teeth.
- "Double teeth" (persistence of temporary teeth).
- Deformed jaws.
- Pointed ears.
- Short neck.
- Long body.
- Roach or hollow back (Lordosis or Kyphosis).
- Steep croup.
- Narrow chest, flat ribcage.
- Tail: incorrect set-on, short or twisted.

Win or lose – you always take the best dog home with you...

- Short limbs.
- Out at elbow.
- Too close behind.

SEVERE FAULTS
- Narrow skull
- Eyes small, deep set or protruding.
- Long muzzle.
- Under or overshot mouth.
- Patella luxation.

ELIMINATING FAULTS:
- Aggressive or overly shy.

In the UK, the faults are universally classified as a departure from the points outlined in the Breed Standard. In the United States the Chihuahua can be disqualified if he has certain faults, which includes any dog over 6 lbs, or a dog with broken down or cropped ears. Cropped ears have been trimmed to make the ears erect, which is not allowed in the UK for any breed. Other disqualifications include a cropped or bobbed tail – which is a tail that has been docked, and, in longcoats, a coat that is too thin and looks bare.

SUMMING UP
Breeders must strive at all times to avoid obvious conditions or exaggerations which would be detrimental in any way to the health, welfare or soundness of this breed.

If a feature or quality is desirable, it should only be present in the right measure – moderation rather than exaggeration will ensure the health and wellbeing of the breed in generations to come.

HAPPY AND HEALTHY

Chapter 8

A toy breed with real character, the Chihuahua has a good life span that can run well into double figures. A faithful companion and willing friend on a non-conditional basis, he will, however, of necessity rely on you for food and shelter, accident prevention and medication. Above all, a healthy Chihuahua is a happy chap.

There are a few significant genetic conditions that have been recognised in the Chihuahua. They will be covered in depth later in the chapter.

VACCINATION

There is much debate over the issue of vaccination at the moment. The timing of the final part of the initial vaccination course for a puppy and the frequency of subsequent booster vaccinations are both under

scrutiny. An evaluation of the relative risk for each disease plays a part, depending on the local situation.

Many owners think that the actual vaccination is the protection, so that their puppy can go out for walks as soon as he or she has had the final part of the puppy vaccination course. This is not the case. The rationale behind vaccination is to stimulate the immune system into producing protective antibodies, which will be triggered if the patient is subsequently exposed to that particular disease. This means that a further one or two weeks will have to pass before an effective level of protection will have developed.

Vaccines against viruses stimulate longer-lasting protection than those against bacteria, whose effect may only persist for a matter of months in some cases. There is also the

possibility of an individual failing to mount a full immune response to a vaccination: although the vaccine schedule may have been followed as recommended, that particular dog remains vulnerable.

A dog's level of protection against rabies, as demonstrated by the antibody titre in a blood sample, is routinely tested in the UK in order to fulfil the requirements of the Pet Travel Scheme (PETS). This is not required at the current time with any other individual diseases in order to gauge the need for booster vaccination or to determine the effect of a course of vaccines; instead, your veterinary surgeon will advise a protocol based upon the vaccines available, local disease prevalence, and the lifestyle of you and your dog.

It is worth remembering that maintaining a fully effective level of immune protection against the disease appropriate to your locale is vital: these are serious diseases, which may result in the death of your dog, and some may have the potential to be passed on to his human family (so-called zoonotic potential for transmission). This is where you will be grateful for your veterinary surgeon's own knowledge and advice.

The American Animal Hospital Association laid down guidance at the end of 2006 for the vaccination of dogs in North America. Core diseases were defined as distemper, adenovirus, parvovirus and rabies. So-called non-core diseases are kennel cough, Lyme disease and leptospirosis. A decision to vaccinate against one or more non-core diseases will be based

on an individual's level of risk, determined on lifestyle and where you live in the US.

Do remember, however, that the booster visit to the veterinary surgery is not 'just' for a booster. I am regularly correcting my clients when they announce that they have 'just' brought their pet for a booster. Instead, this appointment is a chance for a full health check and evaluation of how a particular dog is doing. After all, we are all conversant with the adage that a human year is equivalent to seven canine years.

There have been attempts in recent times to reset the scale for two reasons: small breeds live longer than giant breeds, and dogs are living longer than previously. I have seen dogs of

17 and 18 years of age, but to say a dog is 119 or 126 years old is plainly meaningless. It does emphasise the fact, though, that a dog's health can change dramatically over the course of a single year, because dogs age at a far faster rate than humans.

For me as a veterinary surgeon, the booster vaccination visit is a challenge: how much can I find of which the owner was unaware, such as rotten teeth or a heart murmur? Even monitoring bodyweight year upon year is of use, because bodyweight can creep up, or down, without an owner realising. Being overweight is unhealthy, but it may take an outsider's remark to make an owner realise that there is a problem. Conversely, a drop in bodyweight may be the only pointer to an underlying problem.

The diseases against which dogs are vaccinated include:

ADENOVIRUS
Canine adenovirus 1 (CAV-1) affects the liver (hepatitis) and is seen within affected dogs as the classic 'blue eye', while CAV-2 is a cause of kennel cough (see later). Vaccines often include both canine adenoviruses.

DISTEMPER
This disease is sometimes called 'hardpad' from the characteristic changes to the pads of the paws. It has a worldwide distribution, but fortunately vaccination has been very effective at reducing its occurrence. It is caused by a virus and affects the respiratory,

When your Chihuahua goes for his booster, the vet can give him a thorough check-up.

Kennel cough will spread rapidly among dogs that live together.

gastro-intestinal (gut) and nervous systems, so it causes a wide range of illnesses. Fox and urban stray dog populations are most at risk and are usually responsible for local outbreaks.

KENNEL COUGH

Also known as infectious tracheobronchitis, Bordetella bronchiseptica is not only a major cause of kennel cough but also a common secondary infection on top of another cause. Being a bacterium, it is susceptible to treatment with appropriate antibiotics, but the immunity stimulated by the vaccine is therefore short-lived (six to 12 months).

This vaccine is often in a form to be administered down the nostrils in order to stimulate local immunity at the point of entry, so to speak. Do not be alarmed to see your veterinary surgeon using a needle and syringe to draw up the vaccine, because the needle will be replaced with a special plastic introducer, allowing the vaccine to be gently instilled into each nostril. Dogs generally resent being held more than the actual intra-nasal vaccine, and I have learnt that covering the patient's eyes helps greatly.

Kennel cough is, however, rather a catch-all term for any cough spreading within a dog population – not just in kennels, but also between dogs at a training session or breed show, or even mixing in the park. Many of these infections may not be B. bronchiseptica but other viruses, for which one can only treat symptomatically. Parainfluenza virus is often included in a vaccine programme, as it is a common viral cause of kennel cough.

Kennel cough can seem alarming. There is a persistent cough accompanied by the production of white frothy spittle, which can last for a matter of weeks; during this time the patient is highly infectious to other dogs. I remember when it ran through our five Border Collies – there were white patches of froth on the floor wherever you looked! Other features include sneezing, a runny nose, and eyes sore with conjunctivitis. Fortunately, these infections are generally self-limiting, most dogs recovering without any long-lasting problems, but an elderly dog may be knocked sideways by it, akin to the effects of a common cold on a frail, elderly person.

LEPTOSPIROSIS

This disease is caused by *Leptospira interogans*, a spiral-shaped bacterium. There are several natural variants or serovars. Each is characteristically found in one or more particular host animal species, which then acts as a reservoir, intermittently shedding leptospires in the urine. Infection can also be picked up at mating, via bite wounds, across the placenta, or through eating the carcases of infected animals (such as rats).

A serovar will cause actual clinical disease in an individual when two conditions are fulfilled: the individual is not the natural host species, and is also not immune to that particular serovar.

Leptospirosis is a zoonotic disease, known as Weil's disease in humans, with implications for all those in contact with an affected dog. It is also commonly called rat jaundice, reflecting the rat's important role as a carrier. The UK National Rodent Survey 2003 found a wild brown rat population of 60 million, equivalent at the time to one rat per person. Wherever you live in the UK, rats are endemic, which means that there is as much a risk to the Chihuahua living with a family in a town as the Chihuahua leading a more rural lifestyle.

Signs of illness reflect the organs affected by a particular serovar. In humans, there may be a flu-like illness or a more serious, often life-threatening disorder involving major body organs. The illness in a susceptible dog may be mild, the dog recovering within two to three weeks without treatment but going on to develop long-term liver or kidney disease. In contrast, peracute illness may result in a rapid deterioration and death following an initial malaise and fever. There may also be anorexia, vomiting, diarrhoea, abdominal pain, joint pain, increased thirst and urination rate, jaundice, and ocular changes. Haemorrhage is also a common feature, manifesting as bleeding under the skin, nosebleeds, and the presence of blood in the urine and faeces.

Treatment requires rigorous intravenous fluid therapy to support the kidneys. Being a bacterial infection, it is possible to treat leptospirosis with specific antibiotics, although a prolonged course of several weeks is needed. Strict hygiene and barrier nursing are required in order to avoid onward transmission of the disease.

Annual vaccination is recommended for leptospirosis because the immunity only lasts for a year, unlike the longer immunity associated with vaccines against viruses. There is, however, little or no cross-protection between Leptospira serovars, so vaccination will result in protection against only those serovars included in the particular vaccine used. Additionally, although vaccination against leptospirosis will prevent active disease if an individual is exposed to a serovar included in the vaccine, it cannot prevent that individual from being infected and becoming a carrier in the long-term.

In the UK, vaccines have classically included *L. icterohaemorrhagiae* (rat-adapted serovar) and *L. canicola* (dog-specific serovar). The latter is of especial significance to us humans, since disease will not be apparent in an infected dog but leptospires will be shed intermittently.

The situation in America is less clear-cut. Blanket vaccination against leptospirosis is not considered necessary, because it only occurs in certain areas. There has also been a shift in the serovars implicated in clinical disease, reflecting the effectiveness of vaccination and the migration of wildlife reservoirs carrying different serovars from rural areas, so you must be guided by your veterinarian's knowledge of the local situation.

In affected areas, tick control and vaccination are required to combat Lyme disease.

LYME DISEASE

This is a bacterial infection transmitted by hard ticks. It is restricted to those specific areas of the US where ticks are found, such as the north-eastern states, some southern states, California and the upper Mississippi region. It does also occur in the UK, but at a low level, so vaccination is not routinely offered.

Clinical disease is manifested primarily as limping due to arthritis, but other organs affected include the heart, kidneys and nervous system. It is readily treatable with appropriate antibiotics, once diagnosed, but the causal bacterium, Borrelia burgdorferi, is not cleared from the body totally and will persist.

Prevention requires both vaccination and tick control, especially as there are other diseases transmitted by ticks. Ticks carrying B. burgdorferi will transmit it to humans as well, but an infected dog cannot pass it to a human.

PARVOVIRUS (CPV)

Canine parvovirus disease first appeared in the late 1970s, when it was feared that the UK's dog population would be decimated by it because of the lack of immunity in the general canine population. While this was a terrifying possibility at the time, fortunately it did not happen.

There are two forms of the virus (CPV-1, CPV-2) affecting domesticated dogs. It is highly contagious, picked up via the mouth/nose from infected faeces. The incubation period is about five days. CPV-2 causes two types of illness: gastro-enteritis and

RABIES

This is another zoonotic disease and there are very strict control measures in place. Vaccines were once available in the UK only on an individual basis for dogs being taken abroad. Pets travelling into the UK had to serve six months' compulsory quarantine so that any pet incubating rabies would be identified before release back into the general population. Under the Pet Travel Scheme (PETS), provided certain criteria are met (check the DEFRA website for up-to-date information – www.defra.gov.uk) then dogs can re-enter the UK without being quarantined.

Dogs to be imported into the US have to show that they were vaccinated against rabies at least 30 days previously; otherwise, they have to serve effective internal quarantine for 30 days from the date of vaccination against rabies, in order to ensure they are not incubating rabies. The exception is dogs entering from countries recognised as being rabies-free, in which case it has to be proved that they lived in that country for at least six months beforehand.

heart disease in puppies born to unvaccinated dams, both of which often result in death. Infection of puppies under three weeks of age with CPV-1 manifests as diarrhoea, vomiting, difficulty breathing, and fading puppy syndrome. CPV-1 can cause abortion and foetal abnormalities in breeding bitches.

Occurrence is mainly low now, thanks to vaccination, although a recent outbreak in my area did claim the lives of several puppies and dogs. It is also occasionally seen in the elderly unvaccinated dog.

PARASITES

A parasite is defined as an organism deriving benefit on a one-way basis from another, the host. It goes without saying that it is not to the parasite's advantage to harm the host to such an extent that the benefit is lost, especially if it results in the death of the host. This means a dog could harbour parasites, internal and/or external, without there being any signs apparent to the owner. Many canine parasites can, however, transfer to humans with variable consequences, so routine preventative treatment is advised against particular parasites.

Just as with vaccination, risk assessment plays a part – for example, there is no need for routine heartworm treatment in the UK (at present), but it is vital in the US and in Mediterranean countries.

ROUNDWORMS (NEMATODES)

These are the spaghetti-like worms that you may have seen passed in faeces or brought up in vomit. Most of the deworming treatments in use today cause the adults roundworms to disintegrate, thankfully, so that treating puppies in particular is not as unpleasant as it used to be!

Most puppies will have a worm burden, mainly of a particular roundworm species (Toxocara canis), which reactivates within the dam's tissues during pregnancy and passes to the foetuses developing in the womb. It is therefore important to treat the dam both during and after pregnancy, as well as the puppies.

Professional advice is to continue worming every one to three months. There are roundworm eggs in the environment and, unless you examine your dog's faeces under a microscope on a very regular basis for the presence of roundworm eggs, you will be unaware of your dog having picked up roundworms, unless he should have such a heavy burden that he passes the adults.

It takes a few weeks from the time that a dog swallows a Toxocara canis roundworm egg to himself passing viable eggs (the pre-patent period). These eggs are not immediately infective to other animals, requiring a period of maturation in the environment, which is primarily temperature-dependent and therefore shorter in the summer (as little as two weeks) than in the winter. The eggs can survive in the environment for two years and more.

There are deworming products that are active all the time, which will provide continuous protection when administered as often as directed. Otherwise, treating every month will, in effect, cut in before a dog could theoretically become a source of roundworm eggs to the general population.

It is the risk to human health that is so important: T. canis roundworms will migrate within our tissues and cause all manner of problems, not least of which (but fortunately rarely) is blindness. If a dog has roundworms, the eggs also find

You will need to continue the worming programme started by your puppy's breeder.

their way on to his coat where they can be picked up during stroking. Sensible hygiene is therefore important. You should always carefully pick up your dog's faeces and dispose of them appropriately, thereby preventing the maturation of any eggs present in the fresh faeces.

TAPEWORMS (CESTODES)

When considering the general dog population, the primary source of the commonest tapeworm species will be fleas, which can carry the eggs. Most multi-wormers will be active against these tapeworms. They are not a threat to human health, but it is unpleasant to see the wriggly ricegrain tapeworm

segments emerging from your dog's back passage while he is lying in front of the fire, and usually when you have guests for dinner!

A tapeworm of significance to human health is Echinococcus granulosus, found in a few parts of the UK, mainly in Wales. Man is an intermediate host for this tapeworm, along with sheep, cattle and pigs. Inadvertent ingestion of eggs passed in the faeces of an infected dog is followed by the development of so-called hydatid cysts in major organs, such as the lungs and liver, necessitating surgical removal. Dogs become infected through eating raw meat containing hydatid cysts.

Cooking will kill hydatid cysts, so avoid feeding raw meat and offal in areas of high risk.

There are specific requirements for treatment with praziquantel within 24 to 48 hours of return into the UK under the PETS. This is to prevent the introduction of Echinococcus multilocularis, a tapeworm carried by foxes on mainland Europe, which is transmissible to humans, causing serious or even fatal liver disease.

FLEAS

There are several species of flea, which are not host-specific. A dog can be carrying cat and human fleas as well as dog fleas, but the same flea treatment will kill and/or control them all. It is also accepted that environmental control is a vital part of a flea control programme. This is because the adult flea is only on the animal for as long as it takes to have a blood meal and to

breed; the remainder of the life cycle occurs in the house, car, caravan, shed…

There is a vast array of flea control products available, with various routes of administration: collar, powder, spray, 'spot-on', or oral. Flea control needs to be applied to all pets in the house, regardless of whether they leave the house, since fleas can be introduced into the home by other pets and their human

HEARTWORM (DIROFILARIA IMMITIS)

Heartworm infection has been diagnosed in dogs all over the world. There are two prerequisites: the presence of mosquitoes, and a warm, humid climate.

When a female mosquito bites an infected animal, it acquires D. immitis in its circulating form, as microfilariae. A warm environmental temperature is needed for these microfilariae to develop into the infective third-stage larvae (L3) within the mosquitoes, the so-called intermediate host. L3 larvae are then transmitted by the mosquito when it next bites a dog. Therefore, while heartworm infection is found in all parts of the United States, it is at differing levels. An occurrence in Alaska, for example, is probably a reflection of a visiting dog having previously picked up the infection elsewhere.

Heartworm infection is not currently a problem in the UK, except for those dogs contracting it while abroad without suitable

preventative treatment. Global warming and its effect on the UK's climate, however, could change that.

It is a potentially life-threatening condition, with dogs of all breeds and ages being susceptible without preventative treatment. The larvae can grow to 14 inches within the right side of the heart, causing primarily signs of heart failure and ultimately liver and kidney damage. It can be treated, but prevention is a better plan. In the US, regular blood tests for the presence of infection are advised, coupled with appropriate preventative measures, so I would advise liaison with your veterinary surgeon.

For dogs travelling to heartworm-endemic areas of the EU, such as the Mediterranean coast, preventative treatment should be started before leaving the UK and maintained during the visit. Again, this is best arranged with your veterinary surgeon.

owners. Discuss your specific flea control needs with your veterinary surgeon.

MITES

There are five types of mite that can affect dogs:

Demodex canis: This mite is a normal inhabitant of canine hair follicles, passed from the bitch to her pups as they suckle. The development of actual skin disease or demodicosis depends on the individual. It is seen frequently around the time of puberty and after a bitch's first season, associated with hormonal changes. There may, however, be an inherited weakness in an individual's immune system, enabling multiplication of the mite.

The localised form consists of areas of fur loss without itchiness, generally around the face and on the forelimbs, and 90 per cent will recover without treatment. The other 10 per cent develop the juvenile-onset generalised form, of which half will recover spontaneously. The other half may be depressed, go off their food, and show signs of itchiness due to secondary bacterial skin infections.

Treatment may be prolonged over several months and consists of regular bathing with a specific miticidal shampoo, often clipping away fur to improve access to the skin, together with a suitable antibiotic by mouth. There is also now a licensed 'spot-on' preparation available. Progress is monitored by the examination of

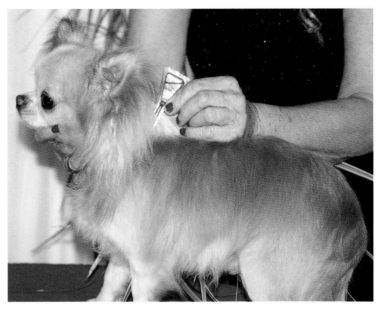

Spot-on treatment is effective in preventing infestation from fleas.

deep skin scrapings for the presence of the mite; the initial diagnosis is based upon abnormally high numbers of the mite, often with live individuals being seen.

Some Chihuahuas may develop the generalised form of demodicosis for the first time in middle-age (more than four years of age). This often reflects underlying immunosuppression by an internal disease, so it is important to identify such a cause and correct it where possible, as well as treating the skin condition.

Sarcoptes scabei: This characteristically causes an intense pruritus or itchiness in the affected Chihuahua, causing

him to incessantly scratch and bite at himself, leading to marked fur loss and skin trauma. Initially starting on the elbows, earflaps and hocks, without treatment the skin on the rest of the body can become affected, with thickening and pigmentation of the skin. Secondary bacterial infections are common.

Unlike Demodex, this mite lives at the skin surface, and it can be hard to find in skin scrapings. It is therefore not unusual to treat a patient for sarcoptic mange (scabies) based on the appearance of the problem even with negative skin scraping findings, and especially if there is a history of contact with foxes, which are a frequent source of the scabies mite.

It will spread between dogs and can therefore also be found in situations where large numbers of dogs from different backgrounds are mixing together. It will cause itchiness in humans, although the mite cannot complete its life cycle on us, so treating all affected dogs should be sufficient. Fortunately, there is now a highly effective 'spot-on' treatment for Sarcoptes scabei.

Cheyletiella yasguri: This is the fur mite most commonly found on dogs. It is often called 'walking dandruff' because it can be possible to see collections of the small white mite moving about over the skin surface. There is excessive scale and dandruff formation, and mild itchiness. It is transmissible to humans, causing a pruritic rash.

Diagnosis is by microscopic examination of skin scrapings, coat combings and sticky tape impressions from the skin and fur. Treatment is with an appropriate insecticide, as advised by your veterinary surgeon.

Otodectes cynotis: A highly transmissible otitis externa (outer ear infection) results from the presence in the outer ear canal of this ear mite, characterised by exuberant production of dark earwax. The patient will frequently shake his head and rub at the ear(s) affected. The mites can also spread on to the

The erect ear carriage of the Chihuahua helps to prevent ear problems.

TICKS

Ticks have become an increasing problem in recent years throughout Britain. Their physical presence causes irritation, but it is their potential to spread disease that causes concern. A tick will transmit any infection previously contracted while feeding on an animal: for example, Borrelia burgdorferi, the causal agent of Lyme disease (see earlier).

The life cycle of the tick is curious: each life stage takes a year to develop and move on to the next. Long grass is a major habitat. The vibration of animals moving through the grass will stimulate the larva, nymph or adult to climb up a blade of grass and wave its legs in the air as it 'quests' for a host on to which to latch for its next blood meal. Humans are as likely to be hosts, so ramblers and orienteers are advised to cover their legs when going through rough long grass.

Removing a tick is simple – provided your dog will stay still. The important rule is to twist gently so that the tick is persuaded to let go with its mouthparts. Grasp the body of the tick as near to your dog's skin as possible, either between thumb and fingers or with a specific tick-removing instrument, and then rotate in one direction until the tick comes away. I keep a plastic tick hook in my wallet at all times.

skin adjacent to the opening of the external ear canal, and may transfer elsewhere, such as to the paws.

When using an otoscope to examine the outer ear canal, the heat from the light source will often cause any ear mites present to start moving around. I often offer owners the chance to have a look, because it really is quite an extraordinary sight! It is also possible to identify the mite from earwax smeared on to a slide and examined under a microscope.

Cats are a common source of ear mites. It is not unusual to find ear mites during the routine examination of puppies and kittens. Treatment options include specific eardrops acting against both the mite and any secondary infections present in the auditory canal, and certain 'spot-on' formulations. It is vital to treat all dogs and cats in the household to prevent recycling of the mite between individuals.

(Neo-) Trombicula autumnalis:

The free-living harvest mite can cause an intense local irritation on the skin. Its larvae are picked up from undergrowth, so they are characteristically found as a bright orange patch on the web of skin between the digits of the paws. It feeds on skin cells before dropping off to complete its life cycle in the environment.

Its name is a little misleading, because it is not restricted to the autumn nor to harvest-time; I find it on the earflaps of cats from late June onwards, depending on the prevailing weather. It will also bite humans.

Treatment depends on identifying and avoiding hotspots for picking up harvest mites, if possible. Checking the skin, especially the paws, after exercise and mechanically removing any mites found will reduce the chances of irritation, which can be treated symptomatically. Insecticides can also be applied – be guided by your veterinary surgeon.

A Z OF COMMON AILMENTS

ANAL SACS (IMPACTED)

The anal sacs lie on either side of the anus at approximately four and eight o'clock, if compared with the face of a clock. They fill with a particularly pungent fluid, which is emptied on to the faeces as they move past the sacs to exit from the anus. Theories abound as to why these sacs should become impacted periodically and seemingly more so in some dogs than others.

The irritation of impacted anal sacs is often seen as 'scooting', when the backside is dragged along the ground. Some dogs will also gnaw at their back feet or over the rump.

Increasing the fibre content of the diet helps some dogs; in others, there is underlying skin disease. It may be a one-off occurrence for no apparent reason. Sometimes an infection can become established, requiring antibiotic therapy, which may need to be coupled with flushing out the infected sac under sedation or general anaesthesia. More rarely, a dog will present with an apparently acute-onset anal sac abscess, which is incredibly painful.

DIARRHOEA

Cause and treatment much as Gastritis (see below).

EAR INFECTIONS

The dog has a long external ear canal, initially vertical then horizontal, leading to the eardrum, which protects the middle ear. If your Chihuahua is shaking his head, then his ears will need to be inspected with an auroscope by a veterinary surgeon in order to identify any cause, and to ensure the eardrum is intact. A sample may be taken from the canal to be examined under the microscope and cultured, to identify causal agents

The responsible owner should acquire a basic knowledge of common canine ailments.

FOREIGN BODIES

Internal: Items swallowed in haste without checking whether they will be digested can cause problems if they lodge in the stomach or obstruct the intestines, necessitating surgical removal. Acute vomiting is the main sign. Common objects I have seen removed include stones from the garden, peach stones, babies' dummies, golf balls and, once, a lady's bra…

It is possible to diagnose a dog with an intestinal obstruction across a waiting room from a particularly 'tucked-up' stance and pained facial expression. These patients bounce back from surgery dramatically. A previously docile and compliant obstructed patient will return for a post-operative check-up and literally bounce into the consulting room.

External: Grass awns are adept at finding their way into orifices such as a nostril, down an ear, and into the soft skin between two digits (toes), whence they start a one-way journey due to the direction of their whiskers. In particular, I remember a grass awn that migrated from a hindpaw, causing abscesses along the way but not yielding itself up until it erupted through the skin in the groin!

before prescribing appropriate eardrops containing antibiotic, antifungal agent and/or steroid. Predisposing causes of otitis externa or infection in the external ear canal include:
- Presence of a foreign body, such as a grass awn
- Ear mites, which are intensely irritating to the dog and stimulate the production of brown wax, predisposing to infection
- Previous infections, causing the canal's lining to thicken, narrowing the canal and reducing ventilation
- Bathing – take great care when bathing your Chihuahua to avoid water entering the ears where it may become trapped and lead to infection. This is a concern in other breeds when swimming, but not for the Chihuahua, who is not generally a keen swimmer!

GASTRITIS

This is usually a simple stomach upset, most commonly in response to dietary indiscretion. Scavenging constitutes a change in the diet as much as an abrupt switch in the food being fed by the owner.

There are also some specific infections that cause more severe gastritis/enteritis, which will require treatment from a veterinary surgeon (see also Canine Parvovirus under 'Vaccination' on page 129).

Generally, a day without food, followed by a few days of small, frequent meals of a bland diet (such as cooked chicken or fish), or an appropriate prescription diet, should allow the stomach to settle. It is vital to ensure the patient is drinking and retaining sufficient water to cover losses resulting from the stomach upset in addition to the normal losses to be expected when healthy. Oral rehydration fluid may not be very appetising for the patient, in which case cooled boiled water should be offered. Fluids should initially be offered in small but frequent amounts to avoid over-drinking, which can result in further vomiting and thereby dehydration and electrolyte imbalances. It is also important to wean the patient back on to routine food gradually or else another bout of gastritis may occur.

JOINT PROBLEMS

It is not unusual for older Chihuahuas to be stiff after exercise, particularly in cold weather. This is not really surprising, given that they are such busy dogs when young. This is such a game breed that a nine- or ten-year-old Chihuahua will not readily forego an extra walk or take kindly to turning for home earlier than usual. Your veterinary surgeon will be able to advise you on ways of helping your dog cope with stiffness, not least of which will be to ensure that he is not overweight. Arthritic joints do not need to be burdened with extra bodyweight!

LUMPS & BUMPS

Regularly handling and stroking your dog will enable the early detection of lumps and bumps. These may be due to infection (abscess), bruising, multiplication of particular cells from within the body, or even an external parasite (tick). If you are worried about any lump you find, have it checked by a veterinary surgeon.

OBESITY

Being overweight does predispose to many other problems, such as diabetes mellitus, heart disease and joint problems. It is so easily prevented by simply acting as your Chihuahua's conscience. Ignore pleading eyes and feed according to your dog's waistline. The body condition is what matters qualitatively, alongside monitoring that individual's bodyweight as a quantitative measure. The Chihuahua should, in my opinion as a health professional, have at least a suggestion of a waist and it should be possible to feel the ribs beneath only a slight layer of fat.

Neutering does not automatically mean that your Chihuahua will be overweight. Having an ovario-hysterectomy does slow down the body's rate of working, castration to a lesser extent, but it therefore means that your dog needs less food. I recommend cutting back a little on the amount of food fed a few weeks before neutering to accustom your Chihuahua to less food. If she looks a little underweight on the morning of the operation, it will help the veterinary surgeon as well as giving her a little leeway weight-wise afterwards. It is always harder to lose weight after neutering than before, because of this slowing in the body's inherent metabolic rate.

The older Chi may develop stiffness in his joints, particularly after exercise.

TEETH

Eating food starts with the canine teeth gripping and killing prey in the wild, incisor teeth biting off pieces of food and the molar teeth chewing it. To be able to eat is vital for life, yet the actual health of the teeth is often overlooked: unhealthy teeth can predispose to disease, and not just by reducing the ability to eat. The presence of infection within the mouth can lead to bacteria entering the bloodstream and then filtering out at major organs, with the potential for serious consequences. That is not to forget that simply having dental pain can affect a dog's wellbeing, as anyone who has had toothache will confirm.

Veterinary dentistry has made huge leaps in recent years, so that it no longer consists of extraction as the treatment of necessity. Good dental health lies in the hands of the owner, starting from the moment the dog comes into your care. Just as we have taken on responsibility for feeding, so we have acquired the task of maintaining good dental and oral hygiene. In an ideal world, we should brush our dogs' teeth as regularly as our own, but the Chihuahua puppy who finds having his teeth brushed is a huge game and excuse to roll over and over on the ground requires loads of patience, twice a day.

There are alternative strategies, ranging from dental chewsticks to specially formulated foods,

Keep a check on your Chihuahua's diet as obesity can lead to major health problems.

but the main thing is to be aware of your dog's mouth. At least train your puppy to permit full examination of his teeth. This will not only ensure you are checking in his mouth regularly but will also make your veterinary surgeon's job easier when there is a real need for your dog to 'open wide!'

INHERITED DISORDERS

Any individual, dog or human, may have an inherited disorder by virtue of the genes acquired from the parents. This is significant not only for the health of that individual but also because of the potential for transmitting the disorder on to that individual's offspring and to subsequent generations, depending on the mode of inheritance.

There are control schemes in place for some inherited disorders. In the US, for example, the Canine Eye Registration Foundation (CERF) was set up by dog breeders concerned about heritable eye disease, and provides a database of dogs who have been examined by diplomates of the American College of Veterinary Ophthalmologists.

To date, only a few conditions have been confirmed in the Chihuahua as being hereditary. In alphabetical order, these include:

COLOUR-DILUTION ALOPECIA

The coat of some blue Chihuahuas becomes sparse and patchy, progressing to alopecia or baldness. The skin is often dry and susceptible to sunburn and secondary bacterial infections.

The mode of inheritance is unclear: it is evidently more than the result of interaction between genes for coat colour since there are blue Chihuahuas with normal coats.

CORNEAL DYSTROPHY

The cornea is the transparent layer across the front of the eye. Corneal dystrophy in the Chihuahua has a late age of onset (six to 13 years of age) and is an inherited, non-inflammatory disorder affecting the inner endothelial layer of the cornea of both eyes. The result is fluid build-up or oedema within the cornea, which becomes cloudy in appearance, often giving the eye a

Breeders strive to eliminate inherited disorders from their breeding programmes.

blue appearance and potentially affecting vision. The affected individual may experience recurrent shallow corneal ulcers, which are painful.

CRYPTORCHIDISM

During foetal development, the testicles form high within the abdomen and migrate down through the abdomen, out along the inguinal canal and into their final position in the scrotum. A dog is said to be cryptorchid if one or both testicles is absent from the scrotum and is instead located within the inguinal canal or within the abdomen. In the Chihuahua, this is thought to be inherited in an autosomal recessive fashion.

CYSTINE UROLITHIASIS

This is a rare inherited problem reported in some surveys of Chihuahuas in the US. There is a defect in the handling of cystine within the kidney, resulting in abnormally high cystine levels in the urine, which predispose to the formation of cystine crystals and stones.

HAEMOPHILIA A

Haemophilia is the most common disorder of blood coagulation, inherited in a sex-linked recessive fashion. This means that the male is either

GLAUCOMA

This is a very painful condition that results from elevated intra-ocular pressure. Untreated, irreversible blindness can develop through damage to the retina and optic nerve. A mode of inheritance is unclear but the Chihuahua is thought to be predisposed to glaucoma secondary to goniodysgenesis, the presence of an abnormal layer of tissue within the drainage angle of the eye.

affected or clear, while females can alternatively be carriers for the trait. Haemophilia A arises from a deficiency of blood-clotting Factor VIII.

There are many ways in which haemophilia A can manifest, at worst as sudden death. There may be early indications, such as prolonged bleeding when the baby teeth are lost or unexpected bruising under the skin. A problem may not become apparent until after surgery such as routine neutering or an injury. Treatment will often require a blood transfusion.

HYDROCEPHALUS

There is an abnormal build-up of fluid within the ventricles (cavities) of the brain, exerting unusual pressure on the brain itself. The mode of inheritance is unknown but there is a breed disposition because of the shape of the Chihuahua's head. This is a relative common congenital abnormality. Severely affected pups will die shortly after birth, while others develop clinical signs before they are three months of age. Mild cases may not be diagnosed until much later.

Signs of hydrocephalus include growth and development falling behind littermates, a pronounced dome to the skull, abnormal movements (such as restless and aimless walking), impaired vision, reduced learning ability (hard to house-train, for example) and seizures.

LEGGE-CALVE-PERTHES DISEASE

Also called Legge-Perthes disease, the problem is more accurately described as an avascular necrosis of the femoral head, meaning the ball of the thigh bone dies before skeletal maturity, resulting in severe pain and lameness apparent from a young age, typically in pups four to six months old. Surgery can be quite effective. Early diagnosis and treatment through pain relief and resting of the affected back leg in a sling may avoid the need for surgical intervention.

PATELLA LUXATION

This is the condition that I point out to my children when I spot a dog walking along the road, giving a little hop for a few steps every now and again. The kneecap or patella is slipping out of position, locking the knee or stifle so that it will not bend, causing the characteristic hopping steps until the patella slips back into its position over the stifle joint. There are various underlying factors. Surgical correction is possible in severely affected dogs, but many simply carry on intermittently hopping, the long-term effect inevitably being arthritis of the stifle.

LYSOSOMAL STORAGE DISEASE

Ceroid lipofuscinosis is a rare condition in the Chihuahua, which gives rise to neurological signs in puppies between the ages of six and 12 months. Inheritance is suspected.

MITRAL VALVE DISEASE

This is a common form of heart disease in dogs more than 10 years old, but the early development of mitral valve disease has been recognised in the Chihuahua. A characteristic heart murmur is an early sign. Once diagnosed, medical therapy can help support the ailing heart, together with ensuring your Chihuahua has regular gentle exercise and does not become overweight.

PATENT DUCTUS ARTERIOSUS (PDA)

This is a common congenital abnormality that may be inherited in the Chihuahua. The ductus arteriosus is a normal feature of the foetus, running from the pulmonary artery to the descending aorta and enabling most of the blood to bypass the lungs during life in the womb; the lungs are not needed for respiration but simply need enough blood for their own development. With the pup's first breath, and by the eighth day of life, this shunt should seal and no longer be patent so that all the blood leaving the right side of the heart is taken to the lungs and thence back to the left side of the heart.

Persistence of the ductus arteriosus adversely affects the cardiovascular system and will ultimately result in heart failure. The characteristic continuous heart murmur may also be felt with the fingers across the chest wall as a so-called 'thrill'. Early diagnosis is essential before clinical signs have developed, enabling surgical intervention in most, but not all, cases.

Another common congenital heart problem, pulmonic stenosis, may be an inherited trait in the Chihuahua.

PATTERN ALOPECIA

Distinct from colour-dilution Alopecia, the affected individual has a normally coloured coat. Patches of thinning and loss of coat become apparent from the age of six to nine months in a symmetrical fashion around the temples of the face, the underside of the neck, on the chest and abdomen, and the backs of the thighs. The underlying skin is not pruritic (itchy) but may darken in colour and become scaly.

TRACHEAL COLLAPSE

Incomplete rings of cartilage help maintain the shape of the windpipe or trachea, providing an easy route for air into and out

Owners are becoming increasingly aware of the benefits of complementary therapies.

of the lungs. Dogs affected with tracheal collapse give a characteristic 'honking' cough as the windpipe collapses on itself during respiration. Excitement, eating and drinking, exercise and pulling while being walked on the lead may increase the tendency, as will enlargement of the heart secondary to heart disease. Obesity can also lead to worsening of the condition. There are various ways of managing this condition, varying from simple actions, such as walking your dog on a harness and avoiding obesity, to specific drugs.

COMPLEMENTARY THERAPIES

Just as for human health, I do believe that there is a place for alternative therapies alongside and complementing orthodox treatment under the supervision of a veterinary surgeon. That is why 'complementary therapies'

Homoeopathy is growing in popularity with vets and owners alike.

is a better name.

Because animals do not have a choice, there are measures in place to safeguard their wellbeing and welfare. All manipulative treatment must be under the direction of a veterinary surgeon who has examined the patient and diagnosed the condition that he or she feels needs that form of treatment. This covers physiotherapy, chiropractic, osteopathy and swimming therapy. For example, dogs with arthritis who cannot exercise as freely as they were accustomed will enjoy the sensation of controlled non-weight-bearing exercise in water, and will benefit with improved muscling and overall fitness.

All other complementary therapies such as acupuncture, homoeopathy and aromatherapy, can only be carried out by veterinary surgeons who have been trained in that particular field. Acupuncture is mainly used in dogs for pain relief, often to good effect. The needles look more alarming to the owner, but they are very fine and are well tolerated by most canine patients. Speaking personally, superficial needling is not unpleasant and does help with pain relief. Homoeopathy has had a mixed press in recent years. It is based on the concept of treating like with like. Additionally, a homoeopathic remedy is said to become more powerful the more it is diluted.

SUMMARY

As the owner of a Chihuahua, you are responsible for his care and health. Not only must you make decisions on his behalf, you are also responsible for establishing a lifestyle for him that will ensure he leads a long and happy life. Diet plays as important a part in this, as does exercise.

For the domestic dog, it is only

in recent years that the need has been recognised for changing the diet to suit the dog as he grows, matures and then enters his twilight years. So-called life-stage diets try to match the nutritional needs of the dog as he progresses through life.

An adult dog food will suit the Chihuahua living a standard family life. There are also foods for those Chihuahuas tactfully termed as obese-prone, such as those who have been neutered or are less active than others, or simply like their food. Do remember, though, that ultimately you are in control of your Chihuahua's diet, unless he is able to profit from scavenging!

On the other hand, prescription diets are of necessity fed under the supervision of a veterinary surgeon because each is formulated to meet the very specific needs of a particular health condition. Should a prescription diet be fed to a healthy dog, or to a dog with a different illness, there could be adverse effects.

It is important to remember that your Chihuahua has no choice. As his owner, you are responsible for any decision made, so it must be as informed a decision as possible. Always speak to your veterinary surgeon if you have any worries about your Chihuahua. He is not just a dog: from the moment you brought him home, he became a member of the family.

With good care and management, your Chihuahua should live a long, happy and healthy life.

THE CONTRIBUTORS

THE EDITOR:
MARGARET GREENING
(HAMAJA)

Margaret Greening acquired her first Chihuahua, Sherry, nearly 50 years ago. Sherry had several puppies in her lifetime and still features far back in pedigrees. She was the starting point of Margaret's Hamaja kennel.

Margaret has kept both longcoats and smoothcoats, but now keeps smoothcoats exclusively. Her Hamaja Kennel has produced Champions both in the UK and abroad, and a number of her Chihuahuas have taken Best of Breed At Crufts in the past. Margaret breeds for excellent temperament as well as physical beauty, placing particular emphasis on friendly and extrovert characteristics.
See Chapter One: Getting To Know Chihuahuas; Chapter Two: The First Chihuahuas; Chapter Three: A Chihuahua For Your Lifestyle; Chapter Seven: The Perfect Chihuahua.

BRENDA HAYES (ARDENVALE)

Brenda has more than 50 years' experience of owning, breeding and keeping show dogs, particularly Chihuahuas. She has judged Chihuahuas at Championship level both in the UK and abroad. She is closely involved with welfare and rescue work and is an animal welfare officer for a public animal centre. Brenda currently runs an avian rescue home.
See Chapter Four: The New Arrival; Chapter Five: The Best of Care.

US CONTRIBUTORS

MARCY ZINGLER (US CONSULTANT)

Marcy L. Zingler was Senior Editor at Howell Book House before joining the AKC staff as Corporate Project Manager. One of her primary responsibilities was as Project Editor for the award-winning AKC 125th Anniversary book. As a freelancer, she was the only outside editor to work on The AKC Complete Dog Book, 20th Edition and 19th Revised.

Marcy's forty-year participation in the dog sport has included breeding, exhibiting, judging, and active leadership in national clubs as officeholder, AKC Delegate and Judges' Education Chair. A three-time National Specialty judge in her original breed, she has judged across the US and in Australia.

Now semi-retired, she again serves as a Delegate to the American Kennel Club.

LINDA GEORGE (OUACHITAH)

Linda George has been breeding and showing Chihuahuas for 40 years using the Ouachitah prefix. She has bred and exhibited many Best in Show, Toy Group, and Specialty winners. Two of her most notable dogs are Ch. Ouachitah For Your Eyes Only, Toy Group winner at Westminster Kennel Club and Ch. Ouachitah Beau Chiene, the breed's Top Producer to date. Linda has held several offices in the Chihuahua Club of America (CCA) and the Chihuahua Club of Greater Milwaukee. She has been a member of the last two Standard revision committees for the CCA and is currently on their Judges' Education committee, having given judges' seminars across the United States.
See Chapter Two: The First Chihuahuas; Chapter Seven: The Perfect Chihuahua.

JULIA BARNES

Julia has owned and trained a number of different dog breeds, and has also worked as a puppy socialiser for Dogs for the Disabled. A former journalist, she has written many books, including several on dog training and behaviour. Julia is indebted to Pat Cullen (Culcia) for her specialist knowledge about Chihuahuas.
See Chapter Six: Training and Socialisation.

ALISON LOGAN MA VetMB MRCVS

Alison qualified as a veterinary surgeon from Cambridge University in 1989, having been brought up surrounded by all manner of animals and birds in the north Essex countryside. She has been in practice in her home town ever since, living with her husband, two children and Labrador Retriever Pippin.

She contributes on a regular basis to *Veterinary Times, Veterinary Nurse Times, Dogs Today, Cat World* and *Pet Patter*, the PetPlan newsletter. In 1995, Alison won the Univet Literary Award with an article on Cushing's Disease, and she won it again (as the Vetoquinol Literary Award) in 2002, writing about common conditions in the Shar-Pei.
See Chapter Eight: Happy and Healthy.

The publishes would also like to thank Pat Milton (Cleopy) and David Milton (Gestavo) for their help and advice in compiling this book.

USEFUL ADDRESSES

KENNEL & BREED CLUBS

UK

The Kennel Club
1 Clarges Street, London, W1J 8AB
Tel: 0870 606 6750
Fax: 0207 518 1058
Web: www.the-kennel-club.org.uk

To obtain up-to-date contact information for the following breed clubs, please contact the Kennel Club:
• British Chihuahua Club
• Chihuahua Club of Scotland
• Chihuahua Club of Wales
• Longcoat Chihuahua Club
• Midland Chihuahua Club
• Northern Counties Chihuahua Club
• Ulster Chihuahua Club
• West Country Chihuahua Club

USA

American Kennel Club (AKC)
5580 Centerview Drive,
Raleigh, NC 27606, USA.
Tel: 919 233 9767
Fax: 919 233 3627
Email: info@akc.org
Web: www.akc.org

United Kennel Club (UKC)
100 E Kilgore Rd, Kalamazoo,
MI 49002-5584, USA.
Tel: 269 343 9020
Fax: 269 343 7037
Web:www.ukcdogs.com/

Chihuahua Club of America, Inc.
Web: www.chihuahuacluboamerica.com/

For contact details of regional clubs, please contact the Chihuahua Club of America.

AUSTRALIA

Australian National Kennel Council (ANKC)
The Australian National Kennel Council is the administrative body for pure breed canine affairs in Australia. It does not, however, deal directly with dog exhibitors, breeders or judges. For information pertaining to breeders, clubs or shows, please contact the relevant State or Territory Controlling Body.

Dogs Australian Capital Teritory
PO Box 815, Dickson ACT 2602
Tel: (02) 6241 4404
Fax: (02) 6241 1129
Email: administrator@dogsact.org.au
Web: www.dogsact.org.au

Dogs New South Wales
PO Box 632, St Marys, NSW 1790
Tel: (02) 9834 3022 or 1300 728 022 (NSW Only)
Fax: (02) 9834 3872
Email: info@dogsnsw.org.au
Web: www.dogsnsw.org.au

Dogs Northern Territory
PO Box 37521, Winnellie NT 0821
Tel: (08) 8984 3570
Fax: (08) 8984 3409
Email: admin@dogsnt.com.au
Web: www.dogsnt.com.au

Dogs Queensland
PO Box 495, Fortitude Valley Qld 4006
Tel: (07) 3252 2661
Fax: (07) 3252 3864
Email: info@dogsqueensland.org.au
Web: www.dogsqueensland.org.au

Dogs South Australia
PO Box 844
Prospect East SA 5082
Tel: (08) 8349 4797
Fax: (08) 8262 5751
Email: info@dogssa.com.au
Web: www.dogssa.com.au

Tasmanian Canine Association Inc
The Rothman Building
PO Box 116
Glenorchy Tas 7010
Tel: (03) 6272 9443
Fax: (03) 6273 0844
Email: tca@iprimus.com.au
Web: www.tasdogs.com

Dogs Victoria
Locked Bag K9
Cranbourne VIC 3977
Tel: (03)9788 2500
Fax: (03) 9788 2599
Email: office@dogsvictoria.org.au
Web: www.dogsvictoria.org.au

Dogs Western Australia
PO Box 1404
Canning Vale WA 6970
Tel: (08) 9455 1188
Fax: (08) 9455 1190
Email: k9@dogswest.com
Web: www.dogswest.com

INTERNATIONAL

Fédération Cynologique Internationalé (FCI)/World Canine Organisation
Place Albert 1er, 13, B-6530 Thuin, Belgium.
Tel: +32 71 59.12.38
Fax: +32 71 59.22.29
Web: www.fci.be/

TRAINING AND BEHAVIOUR

UK

Association of Pet Dog Trainers
PO Box 17, Kempsford, GL7 4WZ
Telephone: 01285 810811
Email: APDToffice@aol.com
Web: http://www.apdt.co.uk

Association of Pet Behaviour Counsellors
PO BOX 46, Worcester, WR8 9YS
Telephone: 01386 751151
Fax: 01386 750743
Email: info@apbc.org.uk
Web: http://www.apbc.org.uk/

USA

Association of Pet Dog Trainers
101 North Main Street, Suite 610
Greenville, SC 29601, USA.
Tel: 1 800 738 3647
Email: information@apdt.com
Web: www.apdt.com/

American College of Veterinary Behaviorists
College of Veterinary Medicine, 4474 Tamu, Texas A&M University
College Station, Texas 77843-4474
Web: http://dacvb.org/

American Veterinary Society of Animal Behavior
Web: www.avsabonline.org/

AUSTRALIA

APDT Australia Inc
PO Box 3122, Bankstown Square, NSW 2200, Australia.
Email: secretary@apdt.com.au
Web: www.apdt.com.au

Canine Behaviour
For details of regional behaviourists, contact the relevant State or Territory Controlling Body.

ACTIVITIES

UK

Agility Club
http://www.agilityclub.co.uk/

British Flyball Association
PO Box 990, Doncaster, DN1 9FY
Telephone: 01628 829623
Email: secretary@flyball.org.uk
Web: http://www.flyball.org.uk/

USA

North American Dog Agility Council
P.O. Box 1206, Colbert,
OK 74733, USA.
Web: www.nadac.com/

North American Flyball Association, Inc.
1333 West Devon Avenue, #512
Chicago, IL 60660
Tel/Fax: 800 318 6312
Email: flyball@flyball.org
Web: www.flyball.org/

AUSTRALIA

Agility Dog Association of Australia
ADAA Secretary, PO Box 2212,
Gailes, QLD 4300, Australia.
Tel: 0423 138 914
Email: admin@adaa.com.au
Web: www.adaa.com.au/

NADAC Australia (North American Dog Agility Council - Australian Division)
12 Wellman Street, Box Hill South, Victoria 3128, Australia.
Email: shirlene@nadacaustralia.com
Web: www.nadacaustralia.com/

Australian Flyball Association
PO Box 4179, Pitt Town, NSW 2756
Tel: 0407 337 939
Email: info@flyball.org.au
Web: www.flyball.org.au/

INTERNATIONAL

World Canine Freestyle Organisation
P.O. Box 350122, Brooklyn, NY 11235-2525, USA
Tel: (718) 332-8336
Fax: (718) 646-2686
Email: wcfodogs@aol.com
Web: www.worldcaninefreestyle.org

HEALTH

UK

Alternative Veterinary Medicine Centre
Chinham House, Stanford in the Vale,
Oxfordshire, SN7 8NQ
Tel: 01367 710324
Fax: 01367 718243
Web: www.alternativevet.org/

British Small Animal Veterinary Association
Woodrow House, 1 Telford Way,
Waterwells Business Park, Quedgeley,
Gloucestershire, GL2 2AB
Tel: 01452 726700
Fax: 01452 726701
Email: customerservices@bsava.com
Web: http://www.bsava.com/

Royal College of Veterinary Surgeons
Belgravia House, 62-64 Horseferry Road,
London, SW1P 2AF
Tel: 0207 222 2001

Fax: 0207 222 2004
Email: admin@rcvs.org.uk
Web: www.rcvs.org.uk

USA

American Holistic Veterinary Medical Association
2218 Old Emmorton Road
Bel Air, MD 21015
Tel: 410 569 0795
Fax 410 569 2346
Email: office@ahvma.org
Web: www.ahvma.org/

American Veterinary Medical Association
1931 North Meacham Road, Suite 100,
Schaumburg, IL 60173-4360, USA.
Tel: 800 248 2862
Fax: 847 925 1329
Web: www.avma.org

American College of Veterinary Surgeons
19785 Crystal Rock Dr, Suite 305
Germantown, MD 20874, USA.
Tel: 301 916 0200
Toll Free: 877 217 2287
Fax: 301 916 2287
Email: acvs@acvs.org
Web: www.acvs.org/

AUSTRALIA

Australian Holistic Vets
Web: www.ahv.com.au/

Australian Small Animal Veterinary Association
40/6 Herbert Street, St Leonards, NSW 2065, Australia.
Tel: 02 9431 5090
Fax: 02 9437 9068
Email: asava@ava.com.au
Web: www.asava.com.au

Australian Veterinary Association
Unit 40, 6 Herbert Street, St Leonards,
NSW 2065, Australia.
Tel: 02 9431 5000
Fax: 02 9437 9068
Web: www.ava.com.au

Australian College Veterinary Scientists
Building 3, Garden City Office Park,
2404 Logan Road, Eight Mile Plains,
Queensland 4113, Australia.
Tel: 07 3423 2016
Fax: 07 3423 2977
Email: admin@acvs.org.au
Web: http://acvsc.org.au

ASSISTANCE DOGS

Canine Partners
Mill Lane, Heyshott, Midhurst,
, GU29 0ED
Tel: 08456 580480
Fax: 08456 580481
Web: www.caninepartners.co.uk
Dogs for the Disabled

The Frances Hay Centre, Blacklocks Hill,
Banbury, Oxon, OX17 2BS
Tel: 01295 252600
Web: www.dogsforthedisabled.org

Guide Dogs for the Blind Association
Burghfield Common, Reading, RG7 3YG
Tel: 01189 835555
Fax: 01189 835433
Web: www.guidedogs.org.uk/

Hearing Dogs for Deaf People
The Grange, Wycombe Road, Saunderton,
Princes Risborough, Bucks, HP27 9NS
Tel: 01844 348100
Fax: 01844 348101
Web: www.hearingdogs.org.uk

Pets as Therapy
3a Grange Farm Cottages, Wycombe Road,
Saunderton, Princes Risborough,
Bucks, HP27 9NS
Tel: 01845 345445
Fax: 01845 550236
Web: http://www.petsastherapy.org/

Support Dogs
21 Jessops Riverside, Brightside Lane,
Sheffield, S9 2RX
Tel: 01142 617800
Fax: 01142 617555
Email: supportdogs@btconnect.com
Web: www.support-dogs.org.uk

USA

Therapy Dogs International
88 Bartley Road, Flanders, NJ 07836,.
Tel: 973 252 9800
Fax: 973 252 7171
Email: tdi@gti.net
Web: www.tdi-dog.o

Therapy Dogs Inc.
P.O. Box 20227, Cheyenne, WY 82003.
Tel: 307 432 0272.
Fax: 307-638-2079
Web: www.therapydogs.com

Delta Society - Pet Partners
875 124th Ave NE, Suite 101 • Bellevue,
WA 98005 USA.
Email: info@DeltaSociety.org
Web: www.deltasociety.org

Comfort Caring Canines
8135 Lare Street, Philadelphia, PA 19128.
Email: ccc@comfortcaringcanines.org
Web: www.comfortcaringcanines.org/

AUSTRALIA

AWARE Dogs Australia, Inc
PO Box 883, Kuranda, Queensland, 488,
Australia.
Tel: 07 4093 8152
Web: www.awaredogs.org.au/

Delta Society — Therapy Dogs
Web: www.deltasociety.com.au